THE WORLD'S BEST PARTY GAMES

Sheila Anne Barry

Illustrated by Doug Anderson

Sterling Publishing Co., Inc.   New York

By the Same Author

Super-Colossal Book of
Puzzles, Tricks & Games

Test Your Wits!

Tricks & Stunts to
Fool Your Friends

The World's Best
Travel Games

Library of Congress Cataloging-in-Publication Data

Barry, Sheila Anne.
  The world's best party games.

  Includes index.
  Summary: Presents instructions for more than 100
easy-to-play party games for all ages.
  1. Entertaining. 2. Games. [1. Games. 2. Parties]
I. Anderson, Doug, 1919–   ill. II. Title.
GV1417.B275   1987   793.2   86-30038
ISBN 0-8069-6482-0
ISBN 0-8069-6483-9 (lib. bdg.)
ISBN 0-8069-6484-7 (pbk.)

Copyright © 1987 by Sterling Publishing Co., Inc.
387 Park Avenue South, New York, N.Y. 10016
Distributed in Canada by Sterling Publishing
℅ Canadian Manda Group, P.O. Box 920, Station U
Toronto, Ontario, Canada M8Z 5P9
Distributed in Great Britain and Europe by Cassell PLC
Artillery House, Artillery Row, London SW1P 1RT, England
Distributed in Australia by Capricorn Ltd.
P.O. Box 665, Lane Cove, NSW 2066
Manufactured in the United States of America

Contents

Before You Begin   5
1. Before the Party   7
2. Icebreakers   19
3. Pairing Off Partners   31
4. Classic Games   39
5. Hilarious Games   61
6. Action Games   79
7. Races for Small Spaces   95
8. Quiet Games   107
    Proverbs & Sayings   125
    Age Range/Index   126

Before You Begin

What makes these games the best party games in the world?

To start with, they're all favorites—surefire, time-tested gems—that delight and excite players at all kinds of parties, from sophisticated adult get-togethers to fast-moving frenzies for 8-year-olds. If you're in doubt about whether a game is appropriate for the kind of party you're planning, check the age-range index at the back of the book.

Few of the games require any preparation. None of them calls for anything special in the way of equipment or supplies. They won't cause any physical damage to your home or your guests. And they won't cause any psychological damage, either. All games have been eliminated that cause hurts or embarassment (keeping anyone as "It" for too long, making anyone the butt of a joke, or pointing up anyone's shortcomings). With these games, *everyone* can have fun.

All the games keep the players involved, whether they're actively participating in a race or a circle game or a challenge of some kind—or laughing their heads off as they watch other players doing absurd things (and waiting their turn).

Some of the games are better known than others, but they all have an appeal—a magic—of their own, and players quickly get captivated by them.

Try selecting a game or two from each chapter when you're planning your party. (Include a couple of extras you can add, if you need them.) By doing that, you're likely to come up with as balanced a program as any you can find.

It's a good idea to have plenty of prizes on hand. They don't have to be expensive or fancy or big. But it helps to make an award. If one person seems to be winning more than a reasonable number of games—and therefore all the prizes—start giving prizes for runners-up. If your budget is tight, you can save by giving out a ticket for each win—or a gold star (you can paste them down on a score card you carry around with you, if you want). Then at the end of the party you can award prizes on the basis of the tickets or the stars (most tickets gets best prize). Another way to do it: put a gift for each person in a grab bag and let the one with the most tickets grab first.

Here, then, are the best party games we've ever played, read about or heard of. May they serve you well!

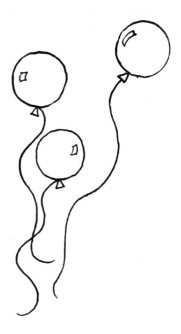

1
Before
the Party

What do you do while your guests are arriving? They don't all show up at the same time, and you don't want to start opening presents or eating food or playing anything major when several guests are still expected. The games in this section are all "fooling around" games that are meant to keep the party going when the party isn't quite ready to get going.

Feelies

Players:	Unlimited
Equipment:	**Covered basket or box**
	A dog biscuit
	A prune
	An onion
	A carrot
	A bracelet
	A piece of string
	A nail
	A wad of tissues
	Any other object with a different kind of feel
	Pencil and paper for each contestant
Preparation:	**Put the objects in the covered basket.**

As your guests arrive, tell them they may slip their hands into the basket—without removing the covering—and feel the objects without looking at them. Let each person feel around under the cover for about a minute. Then provide paper and pencil and ask the player to list the objects in the basket. The person with the most complete correct list wins.

Odd Bean

Players:	**Unlimited**
Equipment:	**12 beans for every player, plus some extras for beans that get lost**
	Small bags (plastic sandwich bags are fine), one for each player
Preparation:	**Measure out the beans, putting 12 in each plastic bag, so you can hand sets to the players as they arrive.**

This game, the 1-2-3-Shoot of beans, is a great one to play before a party starts. People can join it as they arrive, and it can go on as long as you want.

Opening his bag of 12 beans, one player—let's say Gregory—puts a few beans in one fist, stretches it out toward another player and asks, "Odds or evens?" If the other player—Connie—guesses correctly that Gregory's closed fist has an odd number of beans in it, she collects those beans. If she guesses wrong, she has to turn over that many beans to Gregory. The object, of course, is to collect all the beans. When you want to stop playing, the winner is the one with the most beans.

Hul Gul

Players:	**2 or more**
Equipment:	**12 beans for each player (or small stones or nuts or marbles)**
Preparation:	**None**

This ancient game is something like Odd Bean. One

player—let's say David—puts a few beans in one fist and holds it out to Kathy, saying, "Hul gul."

Kathy replies, "Hands full."

David says, "How many?"

Then Kathy has to guess the number of beans in David's hand.

Let's say that David has 8 beans in his hand. Kathy guesses that he has 3. David shows Kathy the 8 beans and says, "Three plus 5 makes 8. Give me 5 beans." Kathy has to give him 5 beans from her supply.

If Kathy had guessed 10 beans, David would have said, "Ten minus 2 is 8. Give me 2 beans."

If Kathy had guessed correctly—8 beans—David would have had to give her all the beans in his hand.

The game goes on until you want to quit. Just have the players count the beans or nuts or stones or marbles that they have left and the one with the most wins. Or you can go on playing until one player has all the beans.

Feather Up! _____

Players:	**Unlimited**
Equipment:	**A feather for each group**
	Watch with a second hand or a stop watch
Preparation:	**None**

How long can you keep a feather up in the air, just by blowing it? Here's your chance to find out. Keep a stop watch or check the second hand of your watch as players try. The one who manages to keep the feather up longest wins.

You can make a full game of this, if you want. Divide the group into 2 or 3 smaller groups. Everyone in each group joins hands while the leaders throw the feathers up in the air. The group that keeps its feather up longest wins.

Balloon Head

Players:	Unlimited—one at a time
Equipment:	Balloons
	Paper and pencil for recording scores
Preparation:	None

How many times can you bounce the balloon off your head without using your hands? The player who hits the balloon the most times (with the head—no arms or shoulders permitted) wins.

Lottery _____

Players:	**Unlimited**
Equipment:	**1. A large glass jar or paper bag of peanuts or dried beans**
	2. An orange (not seedless)
	3. Part of a page of a newspaper
	4. A tall glass of water
	5. A large dictionary
	6. A table lamp
	7. A long piece of string
	8. A photograph of a baby
	9. A small stack of writing paper
	10. A head of lettuce
	Paper and pencil for each player
Preparation:	**Find out the answers to the questions below. Attach a card to each object with the question on it (see below).**

As your guests arrive, give them each a pencil and sheet of paper. Then without touching the objects, each guest is to write down on the page:

1. **The number of peanuts or beans in the jar**
2. **The number of seeds in the orange**
3. **The number of words printed on both sides of the scrap of newspaper**
4. **The quantity of water in the glass**
5. **The number of pages in the dictionary**
6. **The height of the lamp**
7. **The length of the string**
8. **The age of the baby**
9. **The number of sheets in the stack of paper**
10. **The weight of the lettuce**

The winner is the player who guesses closest in the greatest number of classifications.

Elbow-Coin Trick

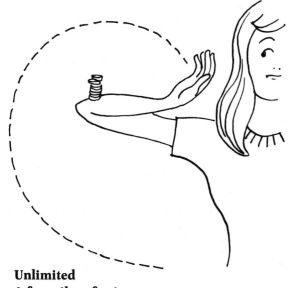

Players: Unlimited
Equipment: A few piles of coins
Preparation: None

This trick takes practice. Few people can do it the first time they try, but it really doesn't take long to get the feel of it. And as a "before the party" game, it's particularly good because more than one person can practice it at a time while you wait for other people to arrive.

Place a pile of coins (start with just one, then 2, then increase to 4 or 5) on your elbow with your hand bent back near your shoulder and your palm open and facing upward. Now bring your hand forward and down sharply in an arc. The coins will fly off your elbow in such a way that your cupped hand can scoop them in with the downward motion before they hit the floor.

Winner is, of course, the person who can catch the most coins.

Card Flip

Players:	**Unlimited**
Equipment:	**A shoe box or a man's hat**
	An old deck of cards (You can use unmatching, incomplete decks. Just put them together so that each player has the same number of cards.)
Preparation:	**None**

Set the open hat (or the shoe box) on the floor from 6 to 10 feet (2 to 3 m) from the door. The door sill is the starting line, and each player must stand on the far side of it. You may not step over the door sill, and if you lean so far over that you lose your balance, you automatically lose.

Each player then flips, snaps, tosses or sails 5 cards, one at a time, trying to get them into the hat. When all the cards have been flipped, count one for each card that got in.

Blind Card Flip

Players:	**Unlimited**
Equipment:	**A shoebox or man's hat**
	An old deck of cards (see "Card Flip")
	A chair
Preparation:	**None**

Place the open hat (or the shoe box) on the floor behind the chair. Then have each player flip, toss or sail a dozen cards, one at a time, over the back of the chair in an attempt to get them in the hat.

Winner is the player who manages to sail the most cards into the hat.

Note: Experiment with the distance you choose to put between the player and the chair and select a space that you're comfortable with. Unless the players are extraordinarily skillful, it doesn't seem to make much difference how close they get to the chair. It's still difficult to get a card into the hat.

Nut Pitching

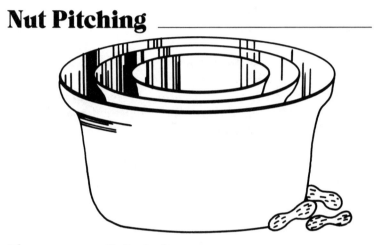

Players:	**Unlimited**
Equipment:	**A bag of nuts (peanuts in the shell are fine)**
	A dishpan
	2 bowls or pans of widely different sizes that will fit into the dishpan
Preparation:	**Set up the bowls, one inside the other, and place both in the dishpan.**

Let players take turns trying to throw three nuts into the center (the smallest) bowl. Putting some water in the larger pans will make the target float, which is interesting! Score 5 points for nuts that are thrown (and stay) in the center bowl, 3 for the larger bowl, 1 for the dishpan. Player with the highest score wins.

Bucket Ball

Players:	Unlimited
Equipment:	Bucket
	Ball
	A couple of books
	Gift wrapping paper (optional)
Preparation:	If you are presenting this game in a carnival atmosphere, put brightly-colored gift wrapping paper around the outside of the bucket. If you want to go further, you can paint a face on the bottom of the bucket, or paste on one from a magazine.

Place the bucket on its side at a slight angle. You can use a book or two to prop it up. A medium-sized ball is about right for this game (see the illustration), and the best distance for throwing is 6 to 10 feet (2 to 3 m). Experiment with this so that the game is not too easy.

Most of the time, when contestants throw the ball, it will bounce right out again after it hits some part of the bucket. You can avoid this, though, if you discover the right spots to hit. For example, if you toss the ball to the left or right side of the bucket at an angle, it will stay in unless you throw it too hard. You will get the same result if the ball hits the lower side of the bucket just beneath the rim. Naturally, no matter where the ball hits, it will bounce, but when it hits a side first it will only bounce around inside the bucket. But don't tell the players that!

Note: Don't use wooden balls. They don't bounce around so much and are much too easy to keep in the bucket.

Blow Gun

Players:	**2 or more**
Equipment:	**A paper straw for each player**
	A supply of used wooden matches (a minimum of 20 or 30)
	Wastebasket
Preparation:	**Cut off the burnt tips from the matches.**

Set up a wastebasket 6 feet (2 m) away from an uneven floorboard or some other spot where people can line up.

Each player gets 10 matches (you can use the same ones over and over again, but have a few extras for ones that get lost).

Then using the straw as a blowgun, shoot the matches into the wastebasket—or try to. Keep track of each player's score. The one with the most wastebasket "hits" wins.

Umbrella Bounce

Players:	Unlimited
Equipment:	An umbrella
	A ball (a rubber ball, a tennis ball, or a Ping Pong ball will do)
Preparation:	None

Open the umbrella and set it upside down on the ground. Mark a starting line about 10 to 15 feet (3 to 5 m) away and use a "live" ball that bounces well.

The object is to bounce the ball into the umbrella so that it *stays* in. You can't toss it in directly—the ball must bounce once.

Each player gets 5 or 10 turns, depending on how many players you have and how much time you want to spend playing this game. Each ball that stays in the umbrella scores one point.

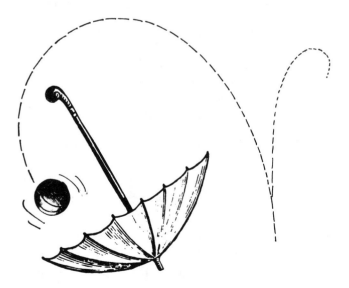

2
Icebreakers

Some icebreakers are "get acquainted" games. Often played at clubs or groups as a way of welcoming new people, they make it easier for unacquainted guests to become part of the group. Others are games that are meant to loosen up a bunch of people so they are relaxed and laughing and ready to take part enthusiastically in whatever games or activities you have planned.

You'll find both types in this section. Also, take a look at Races for Small Spaces on pages 95–108. Almost every one of them is also a super icebreaker!

Blown-Up Fortunes

Players:	5 or more
Equipment:	A balloon for each player, and quite a few extras to substitute for the ones that break ahead of time
	A fortune, written on a slip of paper, for each player
Preparation:	Push a fortune into each balloon.
	Blow up the balloons and tie their mouths.

The fortunes may be funny or serious or silly—anything you think will add to the fun of the party. Here are a few suggestions:

> If you don't stop eating so much cake, you'll get fat.
> You will get a pleasant surprise before the day is out.
> You will marry a robot and have 14 children.
> Watch out for clones.
> You will be a prisoner in the zoo.

You get the idea. When everyone has arrived, throw the balloons up in the air and let the players catch them. After they have each captured a balloon, tell them to burst the balloon if they want to find out their fortunes. The party begins with a BANG.

Zip Zap

Players:	**8 or more**
Equipment:	**None**
Preparation:	**None**

One player volunteers to be the leader and stands in the middle. Then everyone in the circle, going clockwise, takes a turn calling out his or her first and last name. Each person tries to remember the name of the player on the right and left.

Then the leader suddenly points a finger at a player—say Stan—and says slowly, "ZIP—one, two, three, four, five." At this Stan must answer by giving the full name of the player to his left.

If the leader said, "ZAP—one, two, three, four, five," Stan's answer must be the name of the person to his right. If Stan doesn't give the answer before the count of five, then he has missed and becomes "It," while the previous "It" takes Stan's place in the circle.

If Stan gives the right name before the count of five is reached, then "It" remains where he or she is and points to another player. Make it very clear that "ZIP" means the person to the left and "ZAP" is for the person to the right.

Bean Shake

Players:	**10–30**
Equipment:	**10 dried beans for each player**
	A small plastic bag or envelope for each player
Preparation:	**Place the beans in small plastic bags or in envelopes, so that you don't need to take the time to count them out when the party is on.**

Give each player 10 dried beans. Then they are to start shaking hands with each other, over and over, as many times as possible. Why? Because each player gives away a bean to every tenth person he or she shakes hands with. The idea of the game is to get rid of all your beans.

This is a very funny scene, with everyone shaking hands. Of course, while you're trying to get rid of your beans, and handing them out to every tenth person you shake with, you're getting beans back from other shakers!

It's a good idea not to let the players know that they will be your tenth person, because they may try to move away from you. However, no one can refuse to accept a bean if he or she is really the tenth person you shake hands with.

You can also play this game in exactly the opposite way. In the second way, the one who ends up with the *most* beans is the winner. Then everything changes and everyone is anxious and eager to become the tenth player.

First play it one way, then switch to the other. Some of the players will get all mixed up, but it certainly gets everyone acquainted quickly!

Musical Grabs

Players:	**12–30**
Equipment:	**Music (from a tape or record player)**
Preparation:	**None**

The players select partners and then form two circles—one partner in the outer circle and one in the inner circle. "It" stands in the middle, and someone else takes care of the music.

When the music starts, the circles move in opposite directions. When it stops, the circles stop moving, and "It" calls out a command such as "Head to head!" Then the partners have to find each other quickly and put their foreheads together. If "It" can get his or her head together with a partner who hasn't been found yet, "It" becomes that player's partner when the music starts again. The player left without a partner becomes "It," and issues the next command. The fun is in the many possible commands:

Nose to nose
Eye to eye
Cheek to cheek
Foot to foot
Head to toe
Hand in hand
Back to back
Hand to ear
Back to front
Heel to toe
Shoulder to shoulder
Hand to knee

Make up your own!

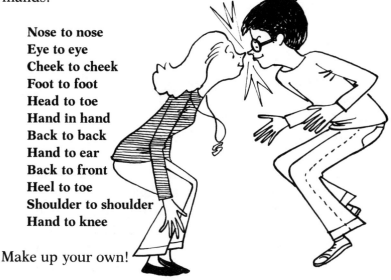

Follow the Leader

Players: **4 or more**
Equipment: **None**
Preparation: **Set up a few "hurdles" in uncrowded places.**

This is a good warmer-upper, and it can be played with any number of players. Be sure to put away breakables beforehand and to point out to the leader the limits of the game—which rooms or parts of the house are out of bounds.

One person is chosen as the leader and the rest of the group must do everything the leader does. It is a good idea to alert the leader beforehand so that he or she can figure out a number of interesting and unusual things to do.

Each player follows the other in a line close behind the leader. If you are in a large area, such as a hall or a gym, the leader can start by making a large circle, and then close in to make a smaller one. Leaders can skip, jump, run or hop or take any other kind of steps. When the circle is small, the leader can unwind it and run in a straight line. The leader can jump over a rope or some hurdles that are set up ahead of time (logs or cartons will do). The leader can do running broad jumps, somersaults and cartwheels.

Almost any activities are fun to do this way. Keep in mind that they should be different from each other and not too hard or too easy for the players.

After this icebreaker, the players will be ready for almost any active game. Depending on the leader, they may be ready for a rest.

This is also a good way to end a party. The leader can pick up papers, carry used dishes out to the kitchen, put on overshoes, and so on, and all the players *must* follow.

Autographs _____

Players:	**5 or more**
Equipment:	**Pencil for each player**
Preparation:	**Type or write a list of your guests and make a copy for each player.**

This is a good way to get your guests acquainted, when most of them are strangers to each other.

Give each player a copy of the guest list. Each person goes around and tries to find out who everyone is. The printed lists of names give them a start. Then they must learn who belongs to each name.

As they do this, the players get each guest to autograph the piece of paper. For example, if one of the names on the list is Kay Robbins, the other guests will have to get Kay to sign after the typed KAY ROBBINS.

The first player to get the complete list of names with correct signatures wins.

Bag on Your Head _____

Players:	**8–30**
Equipment:	**For every player:**
	A large paper bag
	A slip of paper with a number on it
	A safety pin
	A small card or pad
	A pencil
Preparation:	**Write numbers on the slips of paper for the players to pin to their clothes.**

This is another good game to start a party with, if the guests know each other fairly well. As each guest arrives, he or she gets a set of all the equipment listed above. Each player pins the slip with the number to his or her chest, pokes out eye-holes in the paper bag, and slips it on. Then each player tries to guess the names of the other players, who are also wearing bags on their heads. When the players recognize someone, they write that number and name on their card. At the same time, the players try to keep the others from guessing who they are. They try to walk differently or perhaps skip or hop. They may disguise their voices and do many odd things to keep from being recognized.

When all the guests have arrived and the players have finished filling out their cards, ask them to write their own names on the reverse side, and give the card to the person on the right. Read off the correct names and numbers. As the leader reads, the player whose name is called takes off the paper bag. Players total up the correct answers. The one who guessed the most names correctly is, of course, the winner.

Broom Dance

Players:	7 or more
Equipment:	A broom
	Music
Preparation:	None

"The Broom Dance" is always a funny mixer. You need an odd number of people to play and an extra person to start and stop the music.

The players all take partners. (For different ways of pairing up, see pages 31–38.) The extra person dances with the broom. When the music suddenly stops, all the players must change partners. The person with the broomstick drops it and grabs a partner.

The player who is left without a partner picks up the broom and dances with it until the music stops again.

Who Am I? _____

Players:	8 or more
Equipment:	Slips of paper with safety pins on them, one for each player
Preparation:	Write the names of well-known people, living or dead, on the slips of paper.

As the players arrive, pin the slips of paper on their backs without showing them the name on the front. Of course, they can see the names pinned to everyone else's back, but not their own. Then let them try to find out their own identities from each other by asking any question except "What's my name?" Answers can be given only in the form of "Yes" or "No."

Players cannot ask the same person more than one question at a time. They must go from one person to another. When players think they know who they are, they don't say anything, but go to the leader for confirmation.

For example, a player could ask, "Am I a general?" or "Did I fight against England?" and so on, but not "Am I

George Washington?" This type of direct question is saved for the leader, when the player is already fairly sure of the answer. If players guess wrong, they go back to asking questions. After players guess correctly, they re-join the game as answerers.

The leader can keep a record of the order in which players guess their identity and declare the winner later. The game is noisy and funny, because everyone is busy trying to be the first one to find out who he or she is. Players must always answer questions put to them by others.

A word of caution: Cover or remove all mirrors.

Talk Fest

Players:	**4–30**
Equipment:	**Watch with a second hand or a stop watch**
Preparation:	**None**

Divide the group in half and line them up in two rows. Those in one row stand back to back with those in the other row. The players standing back to back become partners.

At a signal, the players turn around quickly and face their partners. They must talk to each other without stopping. They must both talk at the same time—about anything at all—and it doesn't have to make sense! All players must keep this up for 30 seconds.

Sometimes this game is played with only two players talking at a time. They stand in the middle of the room talking fast and furiously while the others watch and laugh. A contest can be set up, and those receiving the most applause are the winners.

Multiplication Dance ⎯⎯⎯⎯⎯⎯

Players:	**8 or more**
Equipment:	**Music**
Preparation:	**None**

Play any kind of dance music, and select 2 players to start off dancing with each other. Then stop the music. The dancers separate and each one selects another partner. The 2 couples dance until the music stops again. Then each one chooses another partner, and 8 people dance. This goes on until everyone is dancing.

You need an even number of players for this ice-breaker. If you have an extra player, he or she can start and stop the music.

3

Pairing Off Partners

Most of the time when people pick partners for some 2-person game, they pick the people who are their closest friends. Often they do it because their friends will be "mad" at them if they don't. And it tends to make a party clique-ish and dull.

Here are a few ways to get people paired off with new partners without anyone's losing face or feeling hurt.

Balloon Buddies

Players:	**8 or more**
Equipment:	**1 balloon for each player**
	Names of players on small slips
Preparation:	**Put a slip bearing the name of a player in each balloon.**
	Blow up the balloons and tie them at the mouths.

When you're ready for the next paired-up game or dance, let the balloons fly and tell the players to take one each. When they burst the balloon, they will find inside it the name of their next partner.

If you want to make sure that you're pairing up boys with girls, use 2 different colors of balloons. Put only boys' names in one color and girls' in the other, and tell the players which color to reach for.

Players get two partners—the one they pick and the one who picks them—enough for two games.

Riddle Pairs

Players:	**8 or more**
Equipment:	**A card for each player**
Preparation:	**Write one line of a riddle on each card.**

Before the pairing-off game, distribute the cards to the players. Their job will be to find the answer—or question—to their riddle. You can stick to well-known riddles if the players are very young, such as "Why did the chicken cross the road?" and "Why do firemen wear red suspenders?" and any others which are particularly familiar to the group. But if the players are older, you can use riddles they've never heard before. Then they will have to find a reasonable answer to the question or a reasonable question for the answer.

Proverb Pairs

Players:	6–20
Equipment:	A card for each player with half a proverb written on it
Preparation:	Write half a proverb on each card.

As each player arrives, or when you are ready for a game that requires partners, hand out the proverb cards to the players. They will find their partners by putting the two parts of the proverb together.

You can play this as a game, if you want. Chop up the proverb into four pieces of paper instead of two, mix them up and put four disjointed parts into an envelope. When your guests arrive, hand them each an envelope. The winners are the players who put together a proverb first.

Note: For a list of familiar proverbs, see page 125.

Clay Mixer

Players:	**8–30**
Equipment:	**Clay or Play-doh, enough to make marble-like balls for half the people at the party**
	Small strips of paper, like fortune cookie strips, one for every girl (or boy) at the party
Preparation:	**Write the names of all the girls at the party (or all the boys) on the fortune cookie strips. Then insert one inside each small piece of clay and round off the clay into a marble-like ball.**

Place the balls in a basket or bowl and when you're ready to pair off partners, let each boy (or each girl) select the ball containing the name of his partner.

Songs

Players:	**6 or more**
Equipment:	**A card for each set of partners with the first line of a song written on it**
Preparation:	**Write up the song line in two sections. Then cut each card so that each half reveals half the first line of the song.**

As the players arrive or when you're ready for the next paired-off game, hand out the song cards to the players. Select songs that are well-known to everyone in the group. The players find their partners by putting the parts of the song together.

Terrible Twosomes

Players: 8 or more
Equipment: A card for each player
Preparation: Write on the cards the names of half of a
                  famous team or couple.

Hand out the cards to the players and stand back while
they try to find the other half of their twosome. You can
use the matching words on page 111 if you prefer, or such
pairs as:

Tom and Jerry
Batman and Robin
Popeye and Olive Oil
Superman and Lois Lane
Abbott and Costello
Captain Kirk and Mr. Spock
Marc Antony and Cleopatra
Jack and Jill
Gilbert and Sullivan
Mutt and Jeff
Oscar and Felix
Napoleon and Josephine
Romeo and Juliet
Kate and Allie
The Devil and the Deep Blue Sea
Laurel and Hardy
Shakespeare and Anne Hathaway
Cinderella and Prince Charming
Hansel and Gretel
Simon and Simon (or Garfunkel or Schuster)

Fish Pond

Players:	**6 or more—an equal number of boys and girls**
Equipment:	**A string with a pencil or other light weight tied to the end for every set of partners**
	A screen (optional)
Preparation:	**Tie the pencils or the weights to the strings.**
	Set up the screen, if you have one, in a corner.

This pairing-off game is also an icebreaker. Start with the girls hiding behind the screen—or, if you don't have a screen, behind a door that is open a few inches.

One boy is given the string with the pencil tied to it. He throws the string over the screen, and without knowing who has thrown it, a girl on the other side grabs the end. Then she becomes his partner.

Each boy gets a turn until all the girls are out from behind the screen or door.

Next time, the boys hide in the "pond" and the girls fish for them.

Split Similes

Players:	**6 or more**
Equipment:	**A card for each player with half a simile on it**
Preparation:	**Write half a simile on each card.**

You can use similes exactly as you used song titles, riddles and twosomes. Give the first part of the simile to one group and the last part to another. Then they need to find each other. Here are some similes to work with:

Blind as a bat	**Bright as a**	**Busy as a bee**
Cold as ice	**penny**	**Dark as night**
Dead as a	**Crazy as a loon**	**Fat as a pig**
doornail	**Fast as greased**	**Fit as a fiddle**
Flat as a	**lightning**	**Happy as a lark**
pancake	**Green as grass**	**Light as a feather**
Hard as a rock	**Heavy as lead**	**Nutty as a**
Mad as a wet	**Neat as a pin**	**fruitcake**
hen	**Playful as a pup**	**Proud as a**
Old as the hills	**Slippery as an**	**peacock**
Scarce as hen's	**eel**	**Slow as molasses**
teeth	**Snug as a bug in**	**Sour as vinegar**
Sly as a fox	**a rug**	**Sweet as honey**
Still as a mouse	**Straight as an**	**(sugar)**
Thin as a rail	**arrow**	

Connections

Players:	**6 or more**
Equipment:	**A card for each player**
Preparation:	**Write name of the person on one set of cards, the object on the other.**

In this system of pairing off, you match up the famous character or person with the object he or she is identified with, such as:

Aladdin	**lamp**
Goldilocks	**porridge**
Cinderella	**glass slipper**
Sleeping Beauty	**spindle**
Rapunzel	**hair**
Jason	**Golden Fleece**
Oliver Twist	**"more" food**
Orville Wright	**plane**
Midas	**gold**
Bo Peep	**sheep**
Miss Muffet	**spider**
Eve	**apple**
Robin Hood	**bow and arrow**
King Arthur	**round table**
Lot's wife	**salt**
Cleopatra	**asp**

If you want to pair up boys and girls, give the boys one list and the girls the other.

4
Classic Games

The great games—the famous ones that have been played (in one variation or another) for a century or more—are still going strong. That's because they work so well. They have a charm and character to them—also an excitement—and they keep players involved. They don't require much (if any) preparation or any special knowledge. You can enjoy playing them whether you all know each other or are strangers, whether you generally prefer quiet games or active ones, whether you're 9 or 90. Here then are some of the favorite games of all time.

Airplane
(a variation on "Pin the Tail on the Donkey")

Players:	8–20
Equipment:	A large map of the world to pin on the wall
	A "plane" cut from light cardboard for each player, with a thumbtack or pushpin in it.
	A blindfold
	A tape measure or ruler
Preparation:	Pin or tape the map to the wall.
	Write the name of a player on each plane.
	Mark a central spot on the map for the takeoff.

Line up the players at the opposite end of the room from the map and put several obstacles in the center of the room (chairs, tables, wastebaskets, etc.). Give each player a minute to study the location of the takeoff spot on the map, and the location of the obstacles before putting on the blindfold. Each player in turn must then cross the floor without touching any of the obstacles and pin the plane on the map as far as possible from the takeoff place. If anyone touches one of the obstacles, it is a crash and the plane is OUT. If the plane is pinned in the water, it is LOST. The pilot of the longest flight wins.

Hot Potato

Players:	**6–30**
Equipment:	**A small potato, ball, stone, or piece of wood**
Preparation:	**None**

The players sit around in a circle facing inwards and one is chosen as leader. The leader steps into the middle of the circle. Then an object, such as a small potato, ball, stone or piece of wood, is passed around from player to player. Each player must accept the object and pass it very quickly.

As the object is passed, the leader closes his or her eyes or turns away. When the leader yells "HOT," the player holding the potato is out. The game is played over and over again until every player but one is out. The last one left in the game is the winner.

If more than 30 want to play, you can form two or more circles. Each circle must have its own potato to pass around, but you need only one leader. The winners from each circle can then form a final circle, to see who is the grand winner.

You can also play this game with music, like Musical Chairs, with the leader stopping the music at intervals.

Truth or Consequences _____

Players:	**6–24**
Equipment:	**A list of questions**
	Supplies for contests
Preparation:	**See individual contests on pages 62–68.**

This game is a great one for young children aged 8 and up—even adults enjoy playing it! It starts with quizzes where you don't have to know anything and ends with a series of contests where you don't have to do too much. But it's a lot of fun.

The leader announces that he or she will be asking a series of questions and if you don't tell the truth you must take the consequences. Then the leader explains that if the players answer the questions correctly that's very good, but they get nothing. However, if they answer wrong, they have to take the consequences and do something, and that may win them a prize.

Then, taking one person at a time, the leader asks a very simple question, such as:

Who is buried in Grant's Tomb?
What color is the sky?
Where do fish live?
What do pigs say?
What do cows say?
What nationality is the President of the
**   United States?**
How many legs has a cat?
How big is a horse?
What makes a car go?
How much is two and two?

At first the players answer correctly, but you as the leader explain that nothing happens that way, and give them another chance. Sometimes they need quite a bit of encouragement to give wrong answers—that Dracula is buried in Grant's Tomb, for example, or that fish live in small huts—but they gradually get the idea. If the answer is wrong, you team them up with another person who gave a wrong answer and select for each twosome a contest from among the ones in this book. (Be sure that the two contestants both like the contest. Especially with young children it is important for them to feel that they are able to do what you're asking of them and want to do it.)

The winner of each contest may then be pitted against another winner, tournament-style, until there is only one grand winner, or you can give prizes to the winners of each separate contest, and to the losers as well.

Note: The contests on pages 62–68 work especially well for "Truth or Consequences," "Forfeits," and other games, or you can just enjoy them for themselves.

Murder

Players:	**6 or more**
Equipment:	**A slip of paper for each player—one with an X on it and one with an O—the rest blank**
Preparation:	**Fold over the slips so that the markings on them cannot be seen and put them in a bowl.**

Tell the players that you're going to play Murder and you'll find everyone wildly enthusiastic. This turns out to be the most popular game at many parties, and that in itself is a mystery!

Each player selects a slip of paper from the bowl, looks at it without letting anyone else see it, and then refolds it carefully and puts it back in the bowl. The player who picked the X is the Murderer and the player who picked the O is the Detective. The Detective leaves the room and waits out in the hall or in the next room. The Murderer says and does nothing.

If the party is taking place at night, now put out the lights. The Murderer goes to someone in the room and puts *one* hand on his or her neck. The Victim screams and falls down dead. At the scream, put the lights back on.

If the party is taking place in the daytime and you cannot get the room dark, don't try. Just let the Murderer "kill" the Victim in full view as everyone sits around on the floor. No one will tell.

Call back the Detective, who is then going to make inquiries and try to find out who-dun-it.

Players don't have to tell the truth about what they were doing. They can say anything they like: that they were out walking the goldfish or asleep on the chandelier or playing chess with Bill Cosby. But guilt will out! Believe it or not, very often the Detective can really tell who did it because culprits look guiltier than the others and give themselves away! The Detective gets three guesses, and as many questions as needed.

Then it is back to the bowl for another round of this game with a new Murderer and Detective and hopefully a new Victim.

If the group is large, it is good to have two detectives. They can confer about their suspicions and it is less lonely. They each get one guess.

In some versions of this game, all players have to tell the truth, except the Murderer. This is all right for parties that take place at night, but many are set in the afternoon when it's light. Since the players are just sitting around, watching the murder, they *can't* tell the truth! And making up silly alibis is half the fun.

Forfeits

Players:	**5–25**
Equipment:	**None**
Preparation:	**None**

Forfeits is an old, old game. It has been popular for centuries because it's such fun.

The players each put a piece of clothing, jewelry or some personal belonging into a pile on the floor. These are the "forfeits." One person is chosen to be the judge, and another holds up the forfeits over the judge's head.

The judge sits in front of the pile and cannot see what is being held overhead. As the sock or necklace or belt is held over the judge's head, the other player says:

"Heavy, heavy hangs over thy head.
What shall the owner do to redeem the forfeit?"

Then the judge (without looking up) commands the owner to do some act or stunt in order to get back the property.

Some ideas for stunts?

1. Try to stand on your head.
2. Answer yes to every question asked by every player in the group.
3. Sing a song.
4. Tell a ghost story.
5. Make at least 3 people laugh.
6. Dance a jig.
7. Walk across the room on your knees.
8. Tell a joke no one in the room has heard.
9. Give a 1-minute talk about elephants.
10. Say five times rapidly: "Three big blobs of a black bug's blood."
11. Say five times rapidly: "Truly rural."
12. Yawn until you make someone else yawn.
13. Holding one foot with your hand, hop around the room.
14. Crawl under the table on all fours and bark like a dog.
15. Tell how to make a pie without talking.
16. Kiss the wall backwards: standing about 20 inches from the wall, lean backwards until your lips touch the wall. Then straighten up without losing your balance. (Take off lipstick first.)
17. Place a basketball in the middle of the floor. Try to sit on it, while writing your name legibly on a card with a pencil.
18. Place 3 strong straightbacked chairs side by side. Lie with your head on the first chair and your feet on the third, with folded arms and stiff body. Have someone

remove the middle chair. Hold your position for 10 seconds.

19. **For 2 players at a time: Both are blindfolded and seated on the floor with a large towel or napkin pinned around the neck like a bib. Each is then given a bowl of popcorn and a spoon and told the feed the other player the entire contents of the bowl. For a messier (and funnier) game, use wheat germ or bran.**

20. **Same setup, but feed each other bananas.**

Of course, the judge and the person who is holding up the forfeit also have articles in the pile, and they must act out a command in order to get them back, too!

Note: For more two-person forfeits, see the contests on pages 62–68.

Horse Race

Players:	3–13
Equipment:	Score sheet, prepared on a large sheet of paper
	A penny for each player
	A deck of cards
Preparation:	Prepare the score sheet as in the diagram, depending on how many "horses" are running in the race.

Prepare your deck, depending on how many people are playing. If you have 13 players, pull out 13 different cards to give out to them—the Ace through the King. If you have only 10 players, don't use the face cards. The suits of these cards should be varied, with an equal number of cards of different suits. For example, with 10 players, you could use the Ace, 2 and 3 of Hearts, the 4 and 5 of Diamonds, the 6, 7 and 8 of Clubs and the 9 and 10 of Spades.

Put the score sheet down flat on the table. Pass out the specially selected cards to the players. They hold on to them so they can remember which cards they have. Then everyone places his or her pennies in the starting box for the card picked.

Shuffle the balance of the deck and turn up one card at a time. Let's say the first card is the 4 of Hearts. The person who received a 4 when you gave out the cards moves his or her penny up one box. But so does anyone else who happens to have a card of the same suit—in this case, a Heart. So in our example, the players with the Ace, 2 and 3 of Hearts would also move up one box.

Turn up the second card and continue the race, until you have a winner.

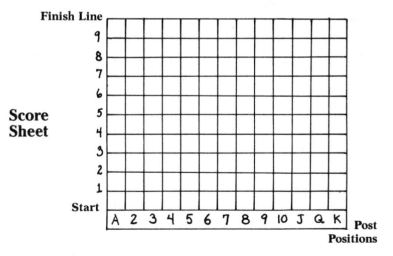

For 13 horses. If you have fewer players, reduce the number of post positions. For example, for 6 players, use Ace through 6.

Charades—"The Game" _____

Players: 10–30
Equipment: Scraps of paper (one for each player)
                Pencils for all
Preparation: None

Charades is a fast and exciting guessing game that you can play in many different ways—with just a few players, with partners, with teams. One player (or more, depending on what version you play) acts out some word or phrase in pantomime while the others guess what it is. The acting-out must be done silently. Code movements can be used—ones that have been agreed on beforehand—but the person doing the acting-out is not allowed to speak.

Divide the group into two teams, each team with a captain. Pass out paper and pencils. The team members are each to write out on their scraps of paper one of the toughest, most un-actable words or quotations or names of movies, plays, books—whatever—they can think of. Then they fold up the scraps of paper, the captain collects them and puts them into a hat or bowl or bag. The captains now trade the scraps of paper, and the race is on.

Each captain rushes back to his or her team and lets the first "actor" select a scrap of paper and proceed to act it out. Both teams may play at the same time, and the first team to guess all the words on the scraps of paper wins. Or, if you prefer, the teams can take turns (see page 55).

Let's say that Gordon is the first actor on his team. He dips into the bag and pulls out the proverb, "A stitch in time saves nine." First he lets his team know that it is a proverb by a pre-arranged signal. You can make up your own signals, but usually a proverb or saying is indicated by bringing up your wrists to shoulder height and wiggling two fingers on each hand to indicate quotation marks.

"Saying!" shouts Sally, one of the players on the team. Gordon nods and points to her.

Then he lets his team know there are six words in the saying by holding up six fingers in a definite motion.

"Six words!" yells Rick, another player on the team.

Gordon nods again. His next decision is which word to act out first. He decides on "stitch." He holds up two fingers.

"Second word," Sally says.

Gordon nods again. He makes believe he is sewing.

"Sewing," Kris says.

Gordon indicates the material in his hand.

"Fabric," says Sally, "cloth—material—"

Gordon tries to indicate a very little stitch on the imaginary material.

"Hole," says Rick, "tear, rip—"

Gordon isn't getting anywhere. He waves his hands back and forth in front of him to stop them and show them that he's going on to something else. He holds up two fingers again.

"Second word, still," says Sally.

Gordon nods. Then he cups his hand to his ear.

"Sounds like," says Anne.

Gordon nods. Then he starts to scratch himself.

"Scratch," yells Kris, "itch—"

Gordon points to her and nods vigorously.

"Itch," says Kris, "sounds like itch—"

"Stitch," yells Rick. Gordon looks insanely happy, points to him and nods. "Stitch," Rick says triumphantly. "The second word is stitch."

Now Gordon holds up four fingers.

"Fourth word," says Sally.

Gordon points to his watch.

"Watch," says Anne, "clock, wrist-watch, what time is it—"

Gordon leaps toward her and points.

"What time is it?" Anne asks.

Gordon points and waves her on.

"Time," shouts Sally.

Gordon swerves and points to her and nods.

"Uh—stitch—uh—time," Sally sums up what they know so far.

At this point, the team will probably guess what Gordon's message is. If they don't he'll probably go ahead to the last word, "nine," which is also easy to act out.

As soon as the team guesses Gordon's charade, the next team member rushes up to collect a charade and act it out.

Charade Signals

Here are some other signals you can work out ahead of time with your team. Most of them are classic signals which are used all over the world by charades players.

Sounds Like: You may have noticed this already in the example when Gordon used "itch" for the word stitch. To do "sounds like," you cup your hand behind your ear.

Book Title: Hold hands up in front of you, as if a book is lying in them.

Film: Put one fist up to your eyes so you can look through it like a camera lens and rotate the other fist in circles as if winding up a handle (like an organ grinder).

Television Show: With one finger of each hand draw a rectangle in the air to indicate a screen.

Play: Indicate an actor by placing one hand on your chest and the other out to the side as if singing.

Song Title: Starting at your open mouth, wiggle the fingers of one hand from there out to the side as if a trill is coming out of your mouth.

Indicate the number of syllables in a word by holding out your left arm and placing fingers of your right hand on your forearm. However many fingers you place on it is the number of syllables in the word.

Indicate which syllable you are going to act out by following this movement with another of the same kind—only this time, if you're acting out the first syllable, only put one finger on your arm—two for the second syllable, and so on.

Indicate small words (articles, conjunctions and prepositions) such as "the," "an," "at," "a," "if," "but," "with," "for," "so" (any small thing)

by holding up your thumb and forefinger about an inch or two apart. Then the team will run through all the small words and won't stop until you point to one of them.

To show the group that the word called was correct, Gordon, in the example, nodded vigorously and pointed. Some people tap the side of the nose instead. Nodding is a more natural thing to do, though, and speeds up the game.

For ideas for charade sayings, see the proverbs and sayings on page 125.

Ways to Play

You don't have to have both teams playing at the same time, though it is a very exciting game if you do. But you miss watching your opponent struggling with the charade you thought up.

If you want, you can let the teams take turns, each player taking as long as necessary to act out the charade, holding a watch on the actor and jotting down the time on the team's score pad.

Or you can give each player a time limit and they either get it or they don't. Decide for yourself how much time to allow. Generally, 3 minutes is long enough. Use a stop-watch—or a kitchen timer.

Up Jenkins!

Players:	12 or more
Equipment:	A long table
	Chairs or benches
	A coin
Preparation:	None

As many players can take part in this game as there are places at the table. Form two teams with an equal number of players and choose a captain for each team. The teams then sit along each side of the table, facing each other. The captains sit at the ends of the table.

The captain of one team gets the coin and passes it under the table to the second person of the team. The players on that team pass the coin under the table back and forth from one player to another. The object of the game is to do it so carefully that the opposing team cannot guess which player has the coin.

At any time, the captain of the opposing team may call out, "Up Jenkins!" At this signal, the players on the team with the coin hold their hands over their heads with their fists clenched. The captain then calls out, "Down Jenkins!" and the players slap their hands with palms flat on the table, keeping the coin hidden under one of the palms. Be careful that there is no clinking sound of the coin when hands are slammed down on the table.

Then the first two players on the opposing team guess which player has the coin. One of them says "Show Up," to the player he or she thinks has the coin. This player must lift up both hands to show if the coin is on the table. If it isn't, the second player gets to guess.

If one of the guesses is right, the opposing team gets a point, and wins a chance to hide the coin. If the guesses both are wrong, the coin stays with the first team, who gets a point. Next time around the third and fourth players on the opposing team get to guess. Set a time limit for play. At that point the team with the most points wins.

In the Manner of the Word _____

Players: **4 or more**
Equipment: **None**
Preparation: **None**

While one player, say Joe, is sent out of the room, the others decide on an adverb which he will have to guess. The clues will be acted out silently by the other players.

Let's say the adverb is "sweetly." When Joe comes back into the room, he asks Susie to do a dance step, for example, "in the manner of the word." Or to walk with a book on her head "in the manner of the word." Or to polish the table—or comb her hair or eat a chocolate or read a magazine—whatever he asks her to do, she must do it "in the manner of the word."

When Susie has executed a dance step reeking with sweetness, Joe asks another player to do the same thing, or a different action. There is no limit to the number of guesses Joe gets, and the game goes on until the adverb is discovered. Then Joe selects a new guesser (preferably the one whose act helped him to guess) and the game goes on.

Be sure to pick adverbs that are easy to act out, such as:

aggressively	hotly	shame-facedly
angrily	hypnotically	sharply
anxiously	impatiently	significantly
bitterly	indifferently	sleepily
brilliantly	jokingly	sneakily
brutally	languorously	softly
charmingly	laughingly	stonily
childishly	lethargically	teasingly
cleverly	lightly	tenderly
clumsily	lovingly	tentatively
coolly	masterfully	timidly
cruelly	mischievously	toughly
daintily	miserably	tremblingly
demurely	murderously	uncomfortably
desperately	nastily	unctuously
eagerly	obsequiously	untidily
flirtatiously	powerfully	venomously
gently	prettily	viciously
gingerly	rambunctiously	wickedly
gratefully	roughly	wisely
hatefully	rudely	wistfully
heavily	sadly	zestfully

In the Manner of the Word with Words

Players:	**4 or more**
Equipment:	**None**
Preparation:	**None**

This game is played just like the last one, but this time, instead of pantomiming something "in the manner of the word," you give a short speech—on any subject that the guesser selects.

For example, let's say the word is "violently." You might be asked to describe your math class "in the manner of the word," or tell about a popular television program, or discuss world peace. The guesser would have no way of knowing, of course, what the word is, and some of the combinations you get can be hilarious!

Another way to play this game is to write the adverbs and subjects for speeches on separate scraps of paper. Put the scraps in separate bowls and let each player take one from bowl A (adverbs) and one from bowl B (speeches). Then, as each person delivers a speech, the others try to guess the adverb which is being acted out.

Here are a few ideas for speeches:

1. **What I Think about Spaghetti**
2. **How to Stand on Your Head**
3. **Famous Cowboys of the East**
4. **Washing Dishes Can Be Fun**
5. **Strange Facts about Alligators**
6. **How to Make Fish Salad**
7. **The Funniest Story I Ever Heard**
8. **Keep an Elephant for a Pet**
9. **How to Carry Peanut Butter in Your Pocket**
10. **The Men (or Women) in My Life**
11. **How to Be Very Very Popular**
12. **I Fought Monsters in Transylvania**
13. **King Kong is My Best Friend**
14. **Karate is Really a Safe Sport**
15. **Insects Don't Bite, You Just Think They Do**

5
Hilarious Games

All the games in this section are wonderfully funny. In every one of them, the players have to do a pretty silly thing (sometimes many silly things) and often keep a straight face while doing it. Don't play these games first at a party. It takes most people a while to get relaxed and feel at ease enough to start laughing. But once they get warmed up with the pre-party games and ice-breakers, they may never stop laughing at these mad, RIDICULOUS, irresistibly funny games.

Baby Bottle Contest

Players:	**2 or more**
Equipment:	**Baby bottles with new nipples, punctured by a straight pin**
Preparation:	**Fill the bottles up to the 1-ounce (28 g) mark with water.**
	Test them to make sure that the water runs out of each bottle at the same speed.

At a signal, each "baby" tries to empty its bottle. The one to finish drinking the water first wins.

This is probably the most popular of all contests. It's hilarious, fast, and everyone loves being a baby again!

Bumble Bee Contest

Players:	**2 or more**
Equipment:	**None**
Preparation:	**None**

Who can buzz longest without taking a breath? Start the contestants together. The first to quit loses.

Grasshopper Contest _____

Players: **2 or more**
Equipment: **None**
Preparation: **None**

Who can hop across the room fastest? First one to hop from the starting line to the opposite wall wins.

Elephant Tug O' War _____

Players: **2 or more**
Equipment: **None**
Preparation: **None**

Select a floorboard or some other line on the floor—the threshold of a door is fine—as the boundary line between the two "elephants." Each elephant (contestant) tries to pull the other one over the line.

One-Legged Contest _____

Players: **2 or more**
Equipment: **None**
Preparation: **None**

Who can stand on one leg longest? Pretty easy and boring, you think? Not necessarily. The rest of the people at the party are allowed to do anything they want to distract the contestants—*except* touch them in any way. That means it is illegal to throw anything at them, too, or hit them with anything. But you can try to make them laugh, make them dizzy, make them *think* you're going to do something that will knock them off balance!

Losing Your Marbles _____

Players: **2 or more**
Equipment: **A dozen marbles**
                 4 saucers or other small plates
                 4 straws
Preparation: **Put 6 marbles on a saucer for each player.**

The object of the contest is to be the first player to move the marbles from one saucer to another—one at a time—with straws. Each player gets two straws and has to use them as chopsticks, picking up one marble at a time and transporting it from one saucer to the other—which is about 5 inches away. If a marble drops to the floor and rolls away, the player has the choice of going after it at that moment or continuing with the marbles in play and hoping the opponent does worse!

Note: It's a good idea to use marbles of different colors for the two players so there are no fights later about whose marble is under the chair and whose is lost!

Blow-Me-Down Race _____

Players: **2 or more**
Equipment: **2 (dry) medicine droppers (the kind that**
                 comes with nose drops—you can get them
                 at a pharmacy)
                 2 small downy feathers (the kind in some
                 sofa pillows) or see below
Preparation: **None**

If you can't get feathers, take 2 rounds of tissue paper about an inch (2.5 cm) in diameter, and pleat them into cones.

Place the feathers or paper puff cones on a smooth-topped table near one edge. The object is to blow them across the table solely by means of air pumped from the medicine droppers. You may not actually touch the droppers to the feathers, but need to use the tiny puffs of air to blow them across. First one to blow his or her feather or paper puff off the opposite side of the table is the winner.

Chimp Race

Players:	**2 or more**
Equipment:	**None**
Preparation:	**None**

Players stand side by side. At a signal, they spread their feet apart, bend over and grasp their ankles. In this position, with knees stiff, they both walk to the goal line, about 20 or 25 feet (6 or 8 m) away. The one who gets there first wins.

If they lose the grip on their ankles, they must return to the starting point and begin again.

This is a super relay race, if you have a large group.

Marshmallow Race

Players:	**2**
Equipment:	**A string about 1½ feet (45 cm) long**
	A marshmallow
Preparation:	**Pull the string through the marshmallow (you can tie it to a skewer and pull it through that way) so that the marshmallow is exactly in the middle of the string.**

Give the players each one end of the same string. They have to chew along the string as rapidly as they can. The one who gets the marshmallow wins and eats it.

Paper Training Race

Players:	**2 or more**
Equipment:	**2 sheets of newspaper for each player (and a few extras in case they tear)**
Preparation:	**None**

In this race you're not allowed to take a step that isn't on newspaper! You start by putting down a sheet of newspaper in front of you and stepping on it. Then you put down the second sheet of paper and step on that—and have to turn around and pick up the first piece of paper and put it down, before you can take another step. Repeat this process all the way to the finish line.

This too is an excellent relay race for a large group.

Cross Parrot Contest

Players: 2 or more
Equipment: None
Preparation: None

The contestants are parrots, angry parrots, who are not permitted to smile. The rest of the people at the party can do anything they'd like to get them to laugh. The parrots are permitted to respond—parrot-style only—if they think they can without cracking up! (No one we ever watched play this game was able to keep from laughing if they tried to talk "parrot.") If you wish, you can make it one of the rules that parrots have to answer questions anyone asks in parrot voices. Last parrot to keep a straight face wins. Lots of fun!

Feeding the Baby

Players:	**4 or more**
Equipment:	**2 glasses of milk**
	2 teaspoons or medicine droppers
	2 bibs or towels
Preparation:	**None**

This contest is similar to the "Baby Bottle Contest," but it is played by two couples—one against the other. A couple, of course, can be a boy and a girl—or two girls or two boys. In any case, one partner feeds the other a small glass of milk, using a teaspoon, one spoonful at a time. The winning team is the first to finish the glass of milk.

Note: Keep the milk glass small and don't fill it all the way to the top. The faster the contest, the more exciting it is.

Ha Ha Ha

Players:	**8–14**
Equipment:	**None**
Preparation:	**None**

Players sit in a circle. The first player says, "Ha." The second player says, "Ha-ha." The third player says, "Ha-ha-ha," and so on, each player adding another "ha." Each "ha" must be pronounced solemnly. If any player laughs or fools around, he or she must drop out of the circle, but once out, anything goes. The eliminated players are free to do anything they can think of to make the other players laugh. No touching allowed.

Hilarious Handkerchief

Players: 6 or more
Equipment: A handkerchief
Preparation: None

The players form a circle. One of them stands in the middle, throws a handkerchief up into the air, and starts laughing. Everyone in the circle laughs, too, until the handkerchief hits the floor. At that moment there is complete silence. Anyone who laughs is out.

Poor Pussy

Players: 5–20
Equipment: None
Preparation: None

This famous game has been popular for generations! The players sit in a circle, except for one person who is "Poor Pussy."

"Poor Pussy"—let's call this unfortunate PP—kneels in front of any player and meows. The person must stroke or pat PP's head and say, "Poor Pussy. Poor Pussy. Poor Pussy," without smiling.

If the person who is petting PP smiles, he or she becomes the next PP, and PP gets to sit in the circle.

It's almost impossible to keep a straight face when you're patting someone's head and saying "Poor Pussy," and to make it even tougher, PP is permitted to do ANYTHING to crack you up, including making weird purring sounds or ridiculous faces or other silly cat-ish moves. Other people in the circle are permitted to laugh, hoot, whistle, and do whatever they can to make it more difficult to keep your cool.

Laughing Ball

Players: 8–20
Equipment: Bouncing ball—any size
Preparation: None

This game is similar to Hilarious Handkerchief, but trickier. The Leader instructs everyone in the circle to start laughing the instant he or she throws the ball into the air. And everyone must keep laughing until someone catches it. At that moment, they have to be absolutely quiet. The one who catches it becomes the Leader for the next round. If anyone doesn't laugh when the ball is in the air, or is caught laughing after the ball is caught, that person must drop out of the circle. To get people out, the Leader can try making some false starts—not quite throwing the ball after making all the motions—not quite catching it after seeming to. If the leader is devious enough, there will soon be a winner!

I Went to the City _____

Players:	8–20
Equipment:	None
Preparation:	None

Players sit in a circle. The Leader says, "I went to the city."

#2 PLAYER: What did you buy?

LEADER: A pair of shoes.

And the Leader moves the feet slightly. The second player repeats the formula to the third and so on around the circle, until all feet are moving. Motions once started must be continued throughout the game. The Leader starts again.

LEADER: I went to the city.

#2: What did you buy?

LEADER: A candy bar (*Chews*).

And so on around the circle with everyone moving feet and chewing.

LEADER: I went to the city.

#2: What did you buy?

LEADER: A hat (*Tips it continuously*).

And so on around the circle, with everyone moving feet, chewing and tipping hat.

LEADER: I went to the city.

#2: What did you buy.?

LEADER: A bustle (*Wiggles*).

And so on around the circle. And so on.

Anyone who doesn't continue all the motions drops out or pays a forfeit (see page 47).

Other objects the Leader can buy:

A dog (get pulled by something on a leash)
A telephone (punch buttons)
A lipstick (put it on)
A razor (shave)
A toothbrush (brush teeth)
A hairbrush (brush hair)
A dumbbell (lift weights)
A cake of soap (wash body)
A smelly sneaker (hold nose)
A hanky (wave it)
An ice cream cone (lick it)

I Took a Trip

Players: 4 or more
Equipment: None
Preparation: None

Everyone sits in a circle. One player, the leader, goes around saying to each player, "I took a trip. What did I take along?" The players name any object they please. One may say, "a suitcase," another says, "a pickle." Other answers might be "a lunch box," "an alarm clock," a peanut butter sandwich," "your poodle."

After each player has named an object, the leader goes around and asks a different question, any kind of question that will be funny, because the players are not supposed to laugh. The leader asks the same question of each player and they each must give the same answer they gave before.

For example, the leader asks something like, "What did I travel on?" The answers would come out, "a suitcase," "a pickle," "a lunch box," and so on. Since anyone who laughs is out of the game, the leader purposely tries to think of questions that will make their answers seem funny and silly.

After everyone has a chance to answer the first question, the leader asks another, such as "What did I wear around my neck?" and then another, trying to get everyone to laugh. The player who laughs last wins.

Monkey See Monkey Do _____

Players: 10–30
Equipment: None
Preparation: None

In this very funny game, none of the players is allowed to laugh. Here's how it goes:

All the players sit close together in a circle. One of them starts the game by turning to the right-hand neighbor and doing something: The player may squeeze the neighbor's arm, muss up hair, straighten clothes, make a face, etc. Whatever that player does, the neighbor must do it to the next player to the right, and that player must do the same thing to the next neighbor.

This goes on all around the circle until it gets back to the first player.

Anyone who laughs is out of the game. Or if you prefer, that person can pay a forfeit to stay in the game. (*See Forfeits on pages 47–48.*)

The player to the right of the first person then has a chance to do something different with the next person, and the game goes on.

This game is more fun if the circle is small. If you're in a large group, try forming a number of circles—10 is a good number for one circle.

Rumor

Players: 8–30
Equipment: Several sheets of paper and pencils
Preparation: None

One of the all-time favorite games, this is a classic. Divide the group into two equal lines or teams. The first players of each team are the captains. They get together and make up a message for both teams. It might be a proverb such as "A bird in the hand is worth two in the bush," or it may be a line from a song, or an original sentence. The original sentence works best.

They write two copies of the message, fold the papers and give one to the last player on each team, who can't look at it. Then the captains go back to the head of their teams.

At a signal, each captain whispers the message to the next player in line—who whispers it to the third player. The message passes from player to player until the last person in line gets the message.

When both teams are finished, the last player of each team says aloud the message he or she has heard. Then they open up the slips of paper and read what the original message was. They are usually quite different. The team that gets the correct message (or the more correct one) wins.

Now the last player becomes the captain and the two new captains decide on another message. The game is played over and over again until everyone has had a chance to make up a message, and to prove that it's not safe to believe any rumor without tracing it back to the source!

Hot Potato Spuds

Players:	**6 or more**
Equipment:	**Potato, ball, stone or piece of wood—** **anything grabbable or passable**
Preparation:	**None**

This terrific game is played just like Hot Potato (page 41), but in this version you are not eliminated when you're caught with the potato. Instead, the next time you get the potato, you have to pass it in a "fancy" way. The leader sets the order.

Here are a few fancy ways to pass potatoes:

1. **Over your head**
2. **Standing**

3. **Standing and turning around and sitting down**
4. **Under your left leg**
5. **Under your right leg**
6. **Around your neck**
7. **Behind your back**
8. **Shaking hands with the next player**
9. **Winking at the next player**
10. **Whistling or singing**
11. **Holding your nose**
12. **Bouncing up and down**

Of course, if you're caught again and again, you gather up your penalties. You have to do the fancy thing you did the first time and then add a new one along with it! When you've been caught several times, it takes you longer to pass the potato than anyone else, naturally, so you're more likely to be caught again! The person who is running the music or the clapping may or may not want to take advantage of you!

Ummm!

Players:	**10 or more**
Equipment:	**A chair for each player except one**
	A blindfold
Preparation:	**Arrange the chairs in a close circle, so people are sitting with their knees tight together and close to the person on either side.**

This great game is actually a grown-up version of "Blind-man's Buff."

Blindfold one player, who is "It." After the blindfold is in place, all the other players take seats in the circle.

"It" walks around the circle and sits down on the lap

of one of the seated players—without touching the seated player in any other way at all.

"It" says "Ummm."

The seated player says "Ummm" (in a disguised voice, of course).

"It" has to try to guess the identity of the seated player. If "It" isn't sure and wants to say "Ummm" again, the seated player must reply with "Ummm" a second time.

"It" gets one more "Ummm" and a reply, and then a third guess. If the guess is correct, the seated player is "It," gets blindfolded, and then everyone changes seats for the next round. If the guess is wrong, "It" goes back into the middle and the game starts again.

Note: Warn the players to disguise their laughter, too.

6
Action Games

Most action games require space. That holds true for many of the games in this section, but almost all can be played indoors in the average apartment or home. Just make sure you put breakables and precious articles away in a safe place before the party starts.

Eggshell Soccer

Players:	4–8
Equipment:	3–4 eggshells (the larger the piece the better)
	A folded paper fan for each player
	4 chairs
Preparation:	Set up the room so that you have an empty playing area in the center of the room. Set up the chairs so they create soccer-type goals at opposite ends of the room.
	Make the paper fans as follows:

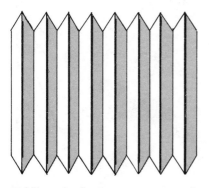

Fold notebook-size paper at 1-inch intervals in opposite directions.

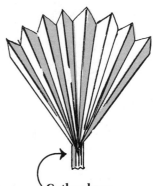

Gather here and staple.

The Leader divides the group into two teams, sending a goalkeeper to each goal. The other players crouch in the middle of the room, each team on its own side of a middle line. One eggshell lies on the line between them.

Then, with the wind they make with their fans, they try to send the eggshell over to the opponent's goal. The only way the goalkeeper can keep the eggshell out is by more ferocious fanning!

If any player actually touches the eggshell, it is a foul and the opponent gets a free whoosh!

Why do you need 3 or 4 eggshells? This silly game can get pretty rough—especially on eggshells. It's good to have spares.

Stalking Bigfoot

Players:	5–20
Equipment	A large table
	2 blindfolds
Preparation:	None

Two players are chosen: one is the Hunter, the other is Bigfoot. Both players are blindfolded and stand at opposite ends of the table.

The Hunter tries to catch Bigfoot, but of course, can't see where Bigfoot is. Bigfoot tries to keep away from the Hunter, but can't tell where the Hunter is. Each tries to fool the other by giving false signals. The Hunter may tiptoe to one end of the table and start pounding and then quickly run to the other end because he expects Bigfoot to run away from the noise. The Hunter may whisper, call out, and give all kinds of misleading signals. Bigfoot also may make sounds and then run to a different spot to fool the Hunter.

The others in the group have fun, too, watching Bigfoot try to escape. Sometimes Bigfoot walks right into the surprised Hunter. You may want to ask those who are watching to be quiet so as not to give any clues, and to stop Bigfoot and the Hunter from running into anything. Or you may want to encourage them to give advice (including misleading advice!) and distract the players. Both ways are interesting.

After the Hunter catches Bigfoot, choose two other players to take their places.

Catching the Snake's Tail _____

Players: **10 or more**
Equipment: **None**
Preparation: **None**

Players line up one behind the other with their arms around the waist of the player in front. The first player— let's say, Donna—has her arms free. She tries to catch the last player on the line—Alex.

The line or "snake" twists and turns while Donna, the Head of the snake, tries to catch Alex, the Tail. Anyone who lets go of the player in front is out. So hang on tight!

When Donna catches Alex, she goes to the end of the line and the second person becomes the head. In that way everyone has a turn at being heads and tails.

Loose Caboose _____

Players:	**10 or more**
Equipment:	**None**
Preparation:	**None**

You need lots of space for this game. Players form groups of three or more. Two people are not in any group, because they will be the loose cabooses.

The groups line up and hold each other's waists. They are the trains that the loose cabooses try to hitch onto. They run around and make sharp turns every time a caboose tries to grab hold of the last player and join the train. If the loose caboose does catch onto a train and can't be shaken loose, the first player of the train becomes a loose caboose.

Sardines

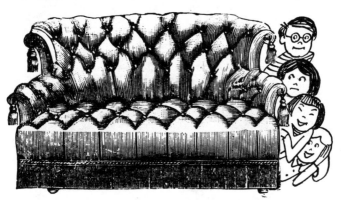

Players:	**5 or more**
Equipment:	**None**
Preparation:	**None**

This is "Hide and Seek" backwards. Only one player hides, and the other players go hunting individually. When a hunter finds the hiding place, though, instead of announcing it, that player gets into the hiding place, too. And so it goes. As each hunter finds the hiding place, the hunter joins the hunted until they are crowded—you guessed it—like sardines. The game goes on until the last hunter finds the sardines.

Steal the Bacon

Players:	**10–30**
Equipment:	**An object such as a ball, Indian club or shoe**
Preparation:	**None**

You need a very large room for this game.

Divide the group in two equal teams. Each team

stands behind a goal line, side by side, and faces the other team. The goal lines should be about 30 feet (10m) apart, if possible. The players on each team count off, each starting at #1. Every player must remember his or her number.

Place the object—the ball, or Indian club, or shoe— in the middle between the two teams. Now the leader calls out a number. The players whose numbers are called (one from each team) run into the middle. They are both trying to "steal" the object and bring it back across their own goal line. When one player snatches it, the other tries to tag him or her before the goal line is reached. If the player with the object succeeds in getting it across the line without being tagged, that team gets one point. If the player is tagged, the other team gets a point. Winning team is the one with the most points in the time you set aside for this game.

The Poisoned Cushions _____

Players: **10–12**
Equipment: **Cushions**
Preparation: **Pile up the cushions in a circle about 5 feet (approximately 2m) in diameter.**

The players stand in a circle around the cushions and clasp hands with each other. The object of the game is to push or pull the other players down onto the "poisoned" cushions, and keep off them yourself. When players touch, step on—or fall into—the poisoned cushions, they are "out," and the circle gets smaller. You may need to remove a few cushions as the circle gets smaller and tighter.

Musical Chairs

Players:	6–40
Equipment:	Chairs, one less than the number of players Music
Preparation:	Line up a row of chairs with alternate chairs facing in opposite directions. If one seat of one chair is facing north, then the seat of the chair next to it should face south.

It's old and familiar, but "Musical Chairs" is still one of the world's best party games, and some marvelous variations on it have been invented, too. Let's start with the basic game.

As soon as the music starts, all the players begin to walk single file around and around the chairs. Suddenly, the music stops. There is a big scramble for seats. One player is left without a seat, and that player must leave the game. Then one chair is taken away, so there is still one chair less than the number of players.

The music starts again. The players walk around and then the music stops. All try to grab seats. The player without a chair leaves the game and another chair is removed.

This goes on until there are just two players walking around one chair. It gets pretty exciting at this point. When the music stops, the player lucky enough to get into the chair wins.

Musical Bumps

Players:	**6 or more**
Equipment:	**Music**
Preparation:	**None**

This "musical chairs" game requires no chairs, just music that the leader plays on a piano, or from a record or tape, or may not play at all—the leader may just clap. The players move to the rhythm. When the leader stops the music or stops clapping, everyone must sit on the floor. The last person to sit is OUT and must go to the sidelines with the leader. For a "sit" to be considered "safe," the contestant's bottom must touch the floor.

Vary the type of music or rhythm so that some is loud, some soft, some fast, some with a jazz beat. Vary the length of each segment, too, so that the players are totally unprepared for the moment the sound stops. Use a few very short segments; they make the game exciting.

If the music is on tape or record, change the volume control suddenly. Many players will sit down at the change in dynamics, without realizing the music is still playing and the game still going on. These players are OUT.

When there are just two players left, they will be busy watching each other and there may be one tie after another, as they both hit the floor at the same time. If this happens, ask them to close their eyes while they move to the music. You'll soon have a winner.

Deep in the Jungle

Players: **12–30**
Equipment: **Enough seats for all but 2 of the players**
Preparation: **None**

This game is similar to Musical Chairs, but it's played with partners. Choose partners using one of the games on pages 32–38. Each set of partners decides to be a particular animal. You could have a pair of monkeys, for example, a pair of anteaters, a pair of lions, and so on.

The partners who don't have chairs (the "It" couple) walk about the room together, saying the names of various jungle animals. When their animal is called, the corresponding partners rise and follow "It" around the room. If the "It" partners say, "The jungle is quiet tonight," *all* players join the line. If the "It" partners say, "The jungle is noisy," everyone runs for the seats. Partners must hold hands as they run and keep holding hands as they sit. This makes for some pretty interesting problems. Of course, the "It" couple tries to get seats, and the unseated couple becomes "It" next time around.

Noah's Ark

In this variation on "Deep in the Jungle," the players can be any living creatures, and the "It" couple calls, "It looks like sunshine" and "It looks like rain."

Musical Islands

Players:	**9–21**
Equipment:	**A sheet of newspaper for every player except one**
Preparation:	**Place the sheets of newspaper on the floor, with one less than the number of players.**

This version of Musical Chairs doesn't require chairs—just "safe" sheets of newspaper. As the music plays the players dance—either with partners or alone, depending on what suits the group. When the music stops, everyone scrambles to find an "island." To get onto an island, you need to stand with one foot and one hand on a sheet of newspaper and hold that position. Anyone who loses his or her balance is out. A sheet of newspaper is then removed for everyone who is out, and the music starts again. The game keeps up until only one player is left, the winner.

Balloon Basketball

Players:	**11–19**
Equipment:	**A generous supply of balloons (10 or 20)**
	Chairs for every player except one
Preparation:	**None**

Set up the chairs in two rows—about 3 feet (1 m) apart—facing each other. Place two of the chairs at either end, between the rows.

"Baskets" stand here ◯ ☐ ☐ ☐ ☐ ☐ ◯ **and here**
                            ☐ ☐ ☐ ☐ ☐

Divide the players into teams. Each team picks a "Basket"—a player who *stands* on the chair at the end of the row. The "Baskets" resemble baskets in shape by making a circle of their arms, with hands clasped together. The other players sit on the chairs.

The referee tosses a balloon into the air in the middle of the rows. The object of the game is for each team to get the balloon through its own Basket, but no one can get up from his or her chair.

The Basket can weave around on the chair and try to capture the balloon, as long is it doesn't move its feet or open its hands.

Each balloon batted through a Basket is worth two points. If the balloon goes out of bounds, the referee tosses another one up from whatever point the balloon went out. After a Basket is scored, the referee starts the play going again by tossing up the balloon at the middle of the rows.

Twenty points wins—or play for a set period of time.

The Circle Test

Players:	**12 or more**
Equipment:	**None**
Preparation:	**None**

The players form a circle, linking elbows. Then all the players step back and pull as hard as they can. The object is to get other players to break the circle. When it finally breaks, the two players whose arms unlinked are out, and the circle forms again, smaller this time, but just as tight. No stopping is allowed, except when the break occurs. If the circle seems invincible, and it doesn't look as if anyone is going to unlink arms, tell everyone to take three steps into the middle of the circle (which relaxes it) and then *quickly* to take three steps back. This snap will often create another break.

Bow Wow

Players:	12–40
Equipment:	None
Preparation:	None

If you play this game indoors, be sure to move back the furniture so you have lots of space.

One player is "It" and all the others stand in a circle, about an arm's length apart.

"It" runs around the outside of the circle, taps one of the players, and keeps running. The tapped player runs around the outside of the circle, in the opposite direction from "It."

When "It" and the tapped paper meet each other running, they must get down on all fours and bark, "Bow Wow," three times. Then they each must get up quickly and continue running around the circle in the same direction as before. The first one to reach the empty space in the circle gets the place. The one left out becomes "It" in the next round.

If the same person is about to be "It" for a third time, choose another "It."

Sherlock and Watson _____

Players: **10–30**
Equipment: **Blindfold**
Preparation: **None**

Everyone joins hands in a circle, except for two players who are inside the circle. One is blindfolded and is called "Sherlock." Sherlock must try to catch the other player, who is called "Watson."

The blindfolded player calls out "Watson!" Then Watson must answer, "Sherlock!" In this way, Sherlock can tell what part of the circle Watson is in. Watson must stay within the circle, and whenever Sherlock says "Watson!" the other must answer "Sherlock!"

When Watson is caught, he or she becomes the blindfolded Sherlock. The previous Sherlock chooses a new Watson and joins the circle. The game continues until everyone has had a turn being Sherlock and Watson.

Numbers Line-Up

Players:	**8–20**
Equipment:	**Paper plates or cards for each player**
	Red and blue crayons
	String or tape
Preparation:	**Write numbers on the back of the plates.**
	Use different colors for each team.

You need 2 exactly equal teams of 4 to 10 players for this game. It is best with a large group (18 to 20 players) and, if you're playing indoors, you need a large room for it.

Each person on each team is given a number. If you have 7 players on each team, you will have numbers 0 to 6; if you have 10, use numbers 0 to 9. Give each player a card with his or her number on it.

The teams stand at opposite ends of the room, with a string or tape separating them, drawn across the middle of the area. A leader stands at the line and calls off numbers. The leader might call "Four hundred thirty two!" At this, the players on each team with cards numbered 4, 3 and 2, run to the line. They line up in the right order, holding their cards in front of them. The first team to line up correctly gets one point. The first team to score 15 points wins.

You can make the game harder and more exciting if you have 20 players who are good in math. The leader can call out, "I'm adding these numbers: 2, 5, 9 and 7 and I will subtract 3. Total?" The players on each team can get into a huddle for this, and the first players to run to the answer line with the correct answer win. In this case, the 2 and the 0 stand together to form 20. You can also multiply and divide for variety.

7
Races for Small Spaces

Here is another type of action game, the relay race. These races are challenging and exciting and they keep everyone involved all the time. You can play them indoors or out, but the ones in this section are all great for indoor parties where space is limited.

See "Hilarious Games" for more races.

Orange Race

Players: 8 or more
Equipment: An orange for each team
Preparation: None

This popular icebreaker never fails to win laughs and sometimes develops a contortionist or two.

Start by dividing the group into equal teams, males and females alternating, if possible. The idea is to pass an ordinary orange from one member of the team to the next, right down the line, using your chin and neck alone.

The first person in line tucks the orange under the chin. The next player must remove the orange with his or her own chin and be ready to surrender it to a third chin. First team to pass the orange down the whole line wins.

If the orange falls to the floor, the player with the clumsy chin must pick it up *by chin alone!*

Hair Ribbon Relay _____

Players: 8–48
Equipment: One hair ribbon for each team
Preparation: None

Two equal teams line up single file. The first player in each line has a long hair ribbon.

At a signal, the first player in each line turns around and ties the ribbon, making a bow, on the head of the next player. Then that player takes it off, turns and ties the hair ribbon the head of Player #3. This goes on until the last player unties the ribbon. The first team to finish wins.

A hair ribbon is the funniest object to play this relay with, but you can use other objects of clothing for variety. Try gloves, or a sweater that buttons down the back!

Pinocchio Race _____

Players: 10–20
Equipment: 2 matchbox tops
Preparation: None

Divide the group into two teams. The object of the game is to pass the matchbox top from player to player, but you're not allowed to touch it with your hands. You have to pass it on your nose. If the matchbox drops, the player who had the matchbox last may pick it up by hand; otherwise, no touching. First team to get the matchbox all the way to the back of the line and forward again wins.

Fancy Dude Relay _____

Players: 6–30
Equipment: 2 assortments of old clothes, with similar articles in them (one for each team)
Preparation: None

Similar to the "Suitcase Relay," this race requires dressing up, but instead of dressing yourself, you dress the team captain.

Divide the group into equal teams. Each team chooses a captain who stands about 20 or 25 feet (6 or 8 meters) away. At a signal, the first player on each team runs up to the captain and puts a piece of clothing on him or her, such as a hat, shoe, scarf, handbag, umbrella, etc. Then this player runs back and tags the second player on the team.

The second player runs to the captain, adds another article of clothing and runs back to tag the next player. The third player dresses the captain some more and so on, until each member of the team has added an item of clothing. You can imagine what the captain looks like after everyone on the team has had a chance to dress him or her up!

The team that finishes first wins.

Salty Whistle Race _____

Players: **2 or more**
Equipment: **1 salty soda cracker (biscuit) for each player**
Preparation: **None**

Have you ever tried to whistle with your mouth full? Here is a whistle race which is lots of fun.

Any number can take part in the race, but only two people play at one time.

Choose two teams, line them up side by side with the teams facing each other. At a signal, the first member of each team starts eating a salty cracker. When finished eating, that player must whistle the first few notes of a song. Then the next player on the team eats a cracker and whistles a tune.

This goes on until all the players on a team have had a chance to eat a cracker and whistle. The first team to finish wins.

Warning: It's a good idea to have a judge watching to make sure everyone eats the whole cracker and whistles.

Doughnut Despair _____

Players:	**8 or more**
Equipment:	**2 doughnuts (plus a few spares)**
	An ice-cream stick for each player (plus a
	few extras in case of breakage)
Preparation:	**None**

Divide the group into teams of equal number and line them up single file. Arm each player with an ice-cream stick and give each of the leaders a doughnut. The leader spears the doughnut with the ice-cream stick in his or her mouth and tries to pass it to the ice-cream stick of the next player. No hands allowed.

When the doughnut has been passed down the line, stick-to-stick, and reaches the last player, that player runs with ice-cream stick and doughnut to the head of the line, taking the first position in the file. Everybody moves back a step. The doughnut is passed again. Each of the players must carry it, and the first team to finish the whole sequence wins.

If the doughnut should fall from the ice-cream stick, it must be picked up with the stick alone, with no hands touching. You'll find ice-cream sticks are a bit fragile and can't withstand much pressure.

Suitcase Relay

Players: 8–24
Equipment: 2 suitcases of old clothes (one for each team)
Preparation: None

Two teams of equal size line up behind the starting line. Abut 15 feet (5 m) away stand two suitcases full of clothing. The suitcases must contain similar articles of clothing. For instance, if you have a hat, a skirt, a jacket, a tie, a scarf, a belt and a necklace in one suitcase, you must have the same items in the other.

At a signal, the first person on each team runs to the team's suitcase and opens it up. The player dresses in all the clothes in the suitcase, closes the suitcase and runs back to the starting line, carrying the suitcase.

There he or she takes off all the clothes and puts them back in the suitcase, closes it, and runs back to leave it in its original position. Then this player runs back to the team and tags off the second player in line, who goes through the same actions. This continues until every player has had a turn. The team to finish first wins.

Magnetism

Players:	8 or more
Equipment:	A paper straw for each player
	A couple of pieces of cleansing tissue, such as Kleenex
Preparation:	None

This relay produces many laughs. Divide the group into two or more teams. Each player is given a straw. The lead player on each team is also given a small piece of Kleenex or other tissue. By drawing in his or her breath, the leader holds the tissue on the end of the straw and passes it on to the next teammate. The idea is to pass it to each member of the team. If the tissue falls on the floor, it must be picked up the same way, by drawing breath through the straw.

The team that finishes first wins. If only a few people are playing, pass the paper back in reverse order.

The Mechanical Doll Race

Players:	2 or more
Equipment:	None
Preparation:	None

Played with partners, this race can be run as a relay or as a contest between 2 couples.

One partner stands perfectly rigid, as if he or she were a mechanical doll. The other partner lifts the doll's foot and places it forward, walking the "doll" to the goal, one foot at a time. First couple or team to reach the goal and return wins.

William Tell Race

Players: 2 or more
Equipment: An apple for each player or each team
Preparation: None

William Tell shot the apple *off* a head—it's your job to keep it on! At a starting signal, players balance an apple on top of their heads and then walk to the finish line. If the apple falls off, it's back to the starting line! Two can play at a time, or you can work the game in teams.

Fast Lemon

Players:	8 or more
Equipment:	2 pencils and 2 similarly-shaped lemons
Preparation:	None

No, this is not a game with new cars but with real lemons!

Divide the group into two or more equal lines. Give the leader of each line a full-length pencil and a full-grown lemon. As the teams line up single file, mark a starting line and a finish line along the floor (about 20 feet or 6 meters away at the most).

The object of the game is to push the lemon with the pencil along the floor in a straight line—if you can. Each player must push it to the finish line and back to the next teammate in line. The team to finish first wins.

What you discover is that the lemon always keeps rolling, despite a slight wobble. You'll have trouble keeping it in your lane, so be sure the furniture is pushed back.

A hint from experienced lemon-rollers: don't push too fast. This generally causes the lemon to roll the wrong way.

Japanese Crab Race _____

Players: 2–60
Equipment: None
Preparation: None

Have you ever tried to run backwards on all fours? Or on your feet and hands? You can run this race either way— or try to. It's very difficult to race backwards. You lose your sense of direction and even become powerless to guide your movements! But it can be done.

Running this race on all fours, the team members position their toes at the starting point and "knee" backwards to the finish line, whereupon the next team member starts out. Score one point for every team member who gets to the finish line. This race can also be run backwards standing up, with both hands and feet on the floor, if you prefer.

If you want, you can have each racer come all the way back to the starting point again before the next one starts out. In that case, finishing gets one point and returning to "GO" gets another.

All Tied Up _____

Players: 8 or more
Equipment: A ball of soft string for each team (with the same length of string on each)
Preparation: None

This funny relay calls for two teams of 4 or more players. The teams line up side by side and face each other. The first player on each team is given the ball of string. Then at a starting signal, the first player holds onto the end of the string and hands the ball to the next player. The next one holds onto the string and unwinds enough so that he or she can pass the ball along to Player #3. The ball is handed along the line, unrolling as it goes.

When the ball of string gets to the person at the far end of the line, that player hands the ball behind his or her back to the player it just came from. That player passes it back, with each player holding on as well as possible, till it gets to the front of the line. Then Player #1 pulls the string around and starts handing the ball along towards the end of the line again.

You see what's happening? The teams are getting wrapped up by the string. The first team to get wrapped up and use all the string wins.

Now you can have an untying relay with the same rules, as each team tries to untie itself first.

8
Quiet Games

After you've played a few of the action games or relay races, you're only too happy to sit quietly for a while. It's also a good idea to alternate quiet games with active ones, and any of the games in this section will keep everyone interested.

The Buzz Family

Players: **2 or more**
Equipment: **None**
Preparation: **None**

Buzz

In this game the players do nothing but count, starting with "One." But instead of saying any number that has 7 in it, or that is a multiple of 7 (14, 21, 28, 35, 42, etc.), they must say "BUZZ."

A game goes like this: the first person says, "One," the second "Two," the next "Three," and so on until it is someone's turn to say "Seven," but that player must say "BUZZ" instead.

The game should proceed at a good clip, and anyone who doesn't say BUZZ when it should be said, or who says BUZZ when it *shouldn't* be said, is OUT.

Fizz Buzz

FIZZ-BUZZ is more difficult and demands an enormous amount of concentration, but it can be hilarious. Just as 7 (and its multiples) are BUZZ, 5 and its multiples are FIZZ. So a game goes like this:

1, 2, 3, 4, FIZZ, 6, BUZZ, 8, 9, FIZZ, 11, 12, 13, BUZZ, FIZZ, 16, BUZZ, 18, 19, FIZZ, BUZZ, 22, 23, 24, FIZZ, 26, BUZZ, BUZZ, 29, FIZZ, 31, 32, 33, 34, FIZZ-BUZZ, 36, BUZZ, 38, 39, FIZZ, 41, BUZZ, 43, 44, FIZZ, 46, BUZZ, 48, BUZZ, FIZZ (50), FIZZ (51), FIZZ (52), FIZZ (53), FIZZ (54), FIZZ-FIZZ (55), FIZZ-BUZZ (56), FIZZ-BUZZ (57), FIZZ (58), FIZZ (59), FIZZ (60) . . .

You get the idea. Same rules apply.

You can play this game with many variations. One of them is based on 3's and 4's—BUZZ is 3 and FIZZ is 4. But when it comes to multiples, it gets more complicated, as you must call out the factors. Here is a sample game:

1, 2, BUZZ, FIZZ, 5, BUZZ times 2, 7, FIZZ times 2, 9, 10, 11, BUZZ times FIZZ, 13, FIZZ, BUZZ times 5, FIZZ times FIZZ, 17, BUZZ times 6, 19, FIZZ times 5 . . .

And so on. As you go along, you might encounter such fancy items as "BUZZ times BUZZ times FIZZ" (36) or "FIZZ times FIZZ times 2" (32), and others where there is more than one way of saying the number. It's up to you what form you give it, as long as you FIZZ-BUZZ it right.

Rags and Bones

In another variation of "BUZZ," 3 is BUZZ, 5 is RAGS and 7 is BONES. In this game, the count in the 50's goes like this:

RAGS (50), RAGS-BUZZ (51), RAGS (52), RAGS (53), RAGS-BUZZ (54), RAGS-RAGS (55), RAGS-BONES (56), RAGS-BONES-BUZZ (57), etc.

Super-Buzz

Super-Buzz is a fantastic party game. The object is for the crowd (one by one) to count to 100 without an error, using 3 for BUZZ. The catch? The direction of the count switches from clockwise to counter-clockwise every time a player misses. Play it *fast*.

Teakettle

Players: 3–50
Equipment: None
Preparation: None

One of the players—"It"—leaves the room. The rest of the group decides upon some word (a homonym or a homophone) that has at least two different meanings but sounds the same, such as blue (blew) or tide (tied). Let's say the group uses "tide."

When "It" comes back, the people in the group take turns using a sentence with the chosen word, but instead of "tide" or "tied," they each substitute the word "teakettle." "It" must figure out the correct word.

They could use sentences like these:

**The teakettle (tide) came in so fast we were
   almost drowned.**
The two players teakettle (tied) for first place.
The horse was teakettle (tied) to the post.

The game goes on until "It" guesses the word. Then the player whose sentence gave the clue becomes "It," and leaves the room while the group decides on some other words.

Note: In some sentences you need to use the word "teakettle*s*," "teakettle*d*" or "teakettl*ing*." You would do this only if the sentence forced you to add a suffix to the original word. For example, if the words are "bear-bare," you would say, "This is the story of the three teakettles (bear-s)," or "The tiger came through the jungle, teakettling (bare-ing) his teeth at me." But if the words are "bears-bares," you would say, "This is the story of the three little teakettle," etc.

Here are some other homonyms and homophones:

air—ere—heir—e'er	foul—fowl	read—reed
aisle—isle—I'll	fur—fir	red—read
ball—bawl	hall—haul	right—write
base—bass	kid—kid	road—rowed—rode
bear—bare	knead—need	role—roll
beau—bow	led—lead	rough—ruff
board—bored	loan—lone	sale—sail
bolder—boulder	mail—male	scene—seen
bough—bow	mussel—muscle	sea—see
bowl—bowl	new—knew	seam—seem
bread—bred	pail—pale	so—sew—sow
break—brake	pair—pare—pear	stair—stare
canopies—can of peas	pause—paws—pours—pores	suede—swayed
ceiling—sealing		sweet—suite
dear—deer	pennants—penance	tear—tier
die—dye	plane—plain	vain—vein—vane
duck—duck	pole—poll	vale—veil
fair—fare	pour—pore	wail—whale
father—farther	quarts—quartz	waist—waste
faun—fawn	rapped—rapt—wrapped	watch—watch
flue—flu—flew		weather—whether
fly—fly		

Another note: The difference between homonyms and homophones is that homonyms are spelled the same, too (bowl, kid, fly and watch are homonyms. The other words in the list above are homophones.)

Group Art

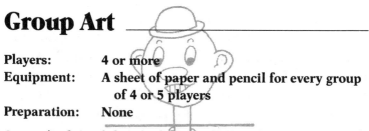

Players:	**4 or more**
Equipment:	**A sheet of paper and pencil for every group of 4 or 5 players**
Preparation:	**None**

So you've heard that nothing really good ever came out of a committee? You haven't played Group Art.

Divide the group into smaller groups of 5 players each (or 4 if that works out better). The first player in each group starts at the top of a page and draws the head of a person and the start of a neck. The player then folds over the paper so that only the last bits of the neck lines are showing and passes the page to the next player, who continues the drawing, finishing the neck, putting in shoulders and arms and completing the drawing all the way down past the waist so that 6 lines are sticking out when the paper is folded and passed: 2 lines for each arm, and 2 lines for hips.

The third player continues the arms and draws in hands, completes the bottom of the subject's torso and draws in the upper legs, leaving 4 lines showing when the paper is folded and passed, all for legs.

The fourth player draws in the knees and calves of the creation, down to the ankles, and the fifth finishes off with shoes. If you want to play with a group of 4, the fourth person can finish off the drawing.

Now unfold the sheet and you have a truly original artistic effort—put together by a group. You see? It isn't true what they say. Groups can come up with greatness.

Group Lit _____

Players:	**5 or more**
Equipment:	**Paper and pencil for each player**
Preparation:	**List of installments, as shown below, or your own variations**

Like Group Art, this game proves that really fine stories can be written by a team. Your team can be 5 to 10 people. If there are more players, divide up into separate teams. But while the team in Group Art may come up with only one drawing, the team in Group Lit will come up with as many stories as there are players!

Each player is going to write a section of the story, as instructed by the Leader, at the top of a sheet of paper. Then the players will fold back the part of the page they wrote on and pass the paper along to the next player, who does the same thing. As you can see, each player is writing on a different sheet for every installment the Leader calls for.

These are some ideas for installments. The Leader can use these or make up new ones.

1. **Write a boy's name and a brief description of him.**
2. **Write a girl's name and a brief description of her.**
3. **Write where they met.**
4. **Where were they supposed to be at the time?**
5. **How they met.**
6. **His first words to her.**
7. **Her first words to him.**

At this point, if you're playing in a team of 7 players, the players get back the papers they started. It doesn't matter—just keep them going around. There can be as many installments as you want—as long as your imagination and the paper hold out.

8. **What happened next.**
9. **What the neighbors said.**
10. **The consequences.**
11. **Where they are now.**
12. **The outlook for the future.**

At the end, unfold the papers and each player reads aloud the story he or she has in hand, putting it all together so it reads smoothly. And there you have it—5, 10, 15, or 20 possible plots for the best-seller lists—or for next season's sitcoms.

This Is My Nose

Players:	**3–30**
Equipment:	**None**
Preparation:	**None**

Everyone lines up facing one of the players, who is "It."

"It" points to a part of its own body, but calls it by some other name. For example, "It" points to a foot and with the other hand points to a player and says. "This is my nose."

Meanwhile, "It" starts counting to 10 and the player who was pointed at must answer before the number 10 is counted. But the player must answer in *reverse*—pointing to his or her own nose and saying "This is my foot."

If the player does not answer "correctly," he or she is out of the game. If the answer is correct, "It" goes on to another player and tries to get that one confused.

"It" may continue by pointing to its own elbow and saying, "This is my knee," and the person "It" points to must then point to his or her own knee and say, "This is my elbow."

Play the game quickly, so that it is hard to keep from getting mixed up.

Guggenheim

Players:	**5 or more**
Equipment:	**Paper and pencil for each player**
Preparation:	**Trace the Guggenheim frame on each sheet and write in the names of categories.**

Guggenheim say: Do not be fooled by apparent simplicity of Guggenheim. Guggenheim easy to play, difficult to win.

Give each player a pencil and the sheet of paper with the Guggenheim framework on it. It should look like this:

	Animal	City	Flower	Food
H				
O				
S				
P				
I				
T				
A				
L				

Leave blanks for each item except the categories (Animal, etc.) and the Guggenheim word (in this case, HOSPITAL). If you don't want to select the word ahead of time, ask the players for an 8- to 10-letter word which will be the Guggenheim subject. Then have them fill in the initial letters of HOSPITAL, as it is filled in here, down the side of the page.

The players get about five minutes to fill in the blanks, without collaboration. You can give them more time, if you want. As the model shows, the first category (Animal) must line up with the first letter of the Guggenheim word, and it must begin with that letter. And so on, down the line.

Players who choose obvious answers, such as those in the illustration, are *not* likely to win. The idea is to get unique items and places to fill in the squares—without consulting a dictionary or atlas or any other book!

	Animal	*City*	*Flower*	*Food*
H	Hyena	Honolulu	Honeysuckle	Ham
O	Ostrich	Oslo	Orchid	Orange
S	Steer	Sydney	Sweet Pea	Spaghetti
P	Pig	Plymouth	Poppy	Pizza
I	Iguana	Indianapolis	Iris	Ice Cream
T	Tiger	Tokyo	Tulip	Toast
A	Alligator	Adelaide	Apple blossom	Apricot
L	Leopard	London	Lily	Lettuce

Keeping Score

The score can be figured in different ways: each player can get a point for the number of people who did *not* write the same word. For example, if you have 15 players, and Burt's word was not repeated by anyone present, Burt would get a score of 15. If two other people wrote down Gerry's word, she would score 13. If six people wrote Min's word, she would get a score of 9. If everyone wrote down Arthur's word, everyone would get 1 point.

Another way to keep score is to give 5 points to any person who has a unique word; 3 points to players whose word was only repeated once, and 1 point to a 3-person word, with no score at all for the others.

The highest number of points wins.

Great Guggenheim

For a super game, choose words with double letters like GUGGENHEIM and BOOKKEEPER and use more column headings, such as Vegetable, Mineral, Nation, Athlete, Actor, Politician, Dessert, Monster, Dog, Author, Cartoon Character, Nursery Rhyme Character, Fairy Tale Character, Hero, River, Mountain, Television Detective, Comedian, Beverage, Emotion, Characteristic, Part of Body, Game, College, City, Flower, Clothing.

Game of the Poet

Players: **2 or more**
Equipment: **Pencil and paper for each player**
Preparation: **None**

This intriguing game was invented by the Parisian poet Dulos in 1648. It became *the* game to play at the French court.

Each player writes four words on a page, the rhyming words of a verse. For example: bad/mad/cheer/here. Then the player passes the page to the player to the right.

That person needs to create a poem from those words. For example:

When I got here
The news was bad.
No smiles, no cheer
So I went mad.

Decide ahead of time just how long you want each round to take. You can make the game fast allowing just a couple of minutes, or schedule more time. Faster is more fun.

Only completed poems score, each line counting 10 points for the poet. If you want, you can allow couplets to score as well. For example:

I thought that I was going mad
But that was really not so bad. = 20 points.

Player who scores the most points in a given number of rounds, wins.

Bad Words

Players: 2 or more
Equipment: None
Preparation: None

"It" leaves the room while the rest decide on a "bad" word. The "bad" word can be anything—"hat," "nose," "running," "beautiful," "quickly"—any part of speech.

When "It" returns, the others ask questions designed to trap "It" into using the "bad" word as often as possible in whatever time period you decide on (3 minutes is good).

Let's say the word is "three." Questions that might force "It" to use the word might be:

What time do you get out of school?
How many bears did Goldilocks meet up with?
How many fingers am I holding up?

One player keeps track of the number of times "It" uses the bad word and each mention scores one point against "It."

Clearly, however, from these questions, "It" is going to realize that the bad word is "three," avoid saying it, and get a very good low score. So the trick is for the players to disguise the conversation so that "It" doesn't realize what's happening and piles up a huge score. They can do this by asking questions that seem to be forcing other words instead, or by asking so many confusing questions that "It" is baffled.

If "It" catches on and guesses the bad word before the end of the turn, "It's" total score is erased. If "It" guesses and is wrong, the score is doubled. Winner is the player with the lowest score after each one has a chance to be "It."

Secret Words _____

Players: **2 or more**
Equipment: **6 index cards (or scraps of paper) and a pencil for each player**
Preparation: **None**

This game is similar to "Bad Words," in that the players try to force their opponents to use a word they have chosen.

Each player writes 6 different words on 6 separate pieces of paper, and turns them face down on the table. Then each player, in turn, asks one of the others a question designed to call forth the secret word. If the opponent uses the secret word, the questioner turns up the paper and leaves it in full view on the table.

Players go on taking turns asking questions until one player turns up all 6 pieces of paper. That one is the winner.

Dictionary

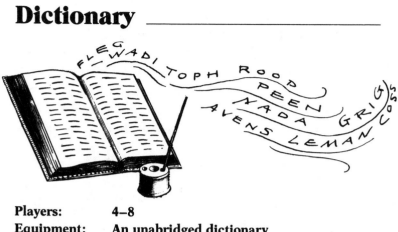

Players:	4–8
Equipment:	**An unabridged dictionary**
	Paper and pencil for scorekeeping
Preparation:	**None**

One player is "It" and looks through the dictionary for a word whose meaning is likely to be unknown to the other players.

Let's say that Charles selects the word "paronymous." He goes on to give a definition of it to the other players. However, he must define it in his own words—not just read it from the dictionary—and the definition he gives them does *not necessarily have to be right.*

Charles might say that "paronymous" means "similar to," for example, and add that it comes from the root, "para," which means "related to." Charles made that up.

The other players have to decide whether or not they believe that Charles has given them a correct definition of the word. Charles gets one point for every player who guesses wrong.

The player to Charles's right goes next.

Note: "Paronymous" is an adjective that refers to words "containing the same root or stem." "Lively" and "life" are "paronymous" words.

Phonies

Players:	**4–12**
Equipment:	**Paper and pencil for each player**
	Small cards or sturdy slips of paper with "difficult" words written on them
Preparation:	**Go through an unabridged dictionary and select a few dozen words that no one in the group is likely to know the meaning of. Write the words, one to a card.**

Pass one card among the players, let them each look at it and figure out for themselves what it means—no looking in dictionaries! Then it is up to them to convince the other players. One by one, each player gives a definition of the word. A good Phonies player may even give a short talk about the word, where it comes from and how he or she just happens to know what it means—such as:

"It's an odd coincidence, I know this word because my Aunt Hannah used to . . ."

It doesn't matter if they're wrong and if they have no idea what the word means. The object of the game is to convince the other players that they know what they're talking about.

Of course, one of them may actually know what the word means but will he or she be as convincing as a talented Phony?

Each player writes the mystery word on the sheet of paper with the definition he or she thinks is correct and the name of the person who gave it. Every time a player's name appears on one of these sheets, it is a point for him or her. Most points wins.

Pass out another card and go through the same process, and another, until you've gone through 10 or so words. The fun comes when you look up the words in the dictionary and find out that all your friends are Phonies. Or are they?

Some words to use:

agnate	**fipple**	**leptorrhine**	**thaumaturgy**
aeromancy	**galangal**	**muticous**	**urticate**
bornan	**hospodar**	**otiose**	**vorant**
deodar	**irade**	**rumal**	**yerk**
epistemic	**jussive**	**subfuscous**	**zarf**

Your dictionary has lots more.

Proverbs & Sayings

You can use the proverbs and sayings in the following list in several of the games in this book, such as Charades or Proverb Pairs.

A bird in the hand is worth two in the bush.
A friend in need is a friend indeed.
A miss is as good as a mile.
A penny saved is a penny earned.
A rolling stone gathers no moss.
A stitch in time saves nine.
A watched pot never boils.
A word to the wise is sufficient.
Absence makes the heart grow fonder.
Actions speak louder than words.
All that glitters is not gold.
An apple a day keeps the doctor away.
April showers bring May flowers.
Beggars can't be choosers.
Birds of a feather flock together.
Blood is thicker than water.
Don't count your chickens until they're hatched.
Don't cry over spilt milk.
Every cloud has a silver lining.
Familiarity breeds contempt.
Half a loaf is better than none.
Handsome is as handsome does.
Haste makes waste.
He who laughs last laughs best.
Heaven helps those who help themselves.
Honesty is the best policy.
Let sleeping dogs lie.
Look before you leap.
Make hay while the sun shines.
Necessity is the mother of invention.
One man's meat is another's man's poison.
Out of the frying pan, into the fire.
Practice makes perfect.
Rome wasn't built in a day.
Spare the rod and spoil the child.
Strike while the iron is hot.
The early bird catches the worm.
The pen is mightier than the sword.
There's no fool like an old fool.
There's no place like home.

Age Range Chart & Index

| | | Ages | | | |
Game	Page	6–8	8–12	13–18	Adult
Airplane	40	★	★	★	★
All Tied Up	105		★	★	★
Autographs	25		★	★	★
Baby Bottle Contest	62	★	★	★	★
Bad Words	120		★	★	★
Bag on Your Head	26		★	★	★
Balloon Basketball	90		★		
Balloon Buddies	32	★	★	★	★
Balloon Head	11	★	★		
Bean Shake	22		★	★	★
Blind Card Flip	14		★	★	★
Blow Gun	17		★	★	★
Blow-Me-Down Race	64		★	★	★
Blown-Up Fortunes	2		★	★	★
Bow-Wow	92		★		
Broom Dance	27			★	★
Bucket Ball	16		★	★	★
Bumble Bee Contest	62	★	★		
Buzz Family	108	★	★	★	★
Card Flip	14		★	★	★
Catching The Snake's Tail	82	★	★	★	★
Charades	50		★	★	★
Chimp Race	65		★		
Circle Test	91		★		
Clay Mixer	34	★	★	★	★
Connections	38		★	★	★
Cross Parrot Contest	67	★	★	★	★
Deep in the Jungle	88		★	★	★
Dictionary	122		★	★	★
Doughnut Despair	98		★	★	★
Eggshell Soccer	80		★		
Elbow-Coin Trick	13		★	★	★
Elephant Tug O' War	63	★	★	★	
Fancy Dude Relay	100	★	★	★	★
Fast Lemon	104	★	★	★	★

AGE RANGE CHART & INDEX

Game	Page	6–8	8–12	13–18	Adult
Feather Up!	10		★	★	★
Feeding the Baby	68		★	★	★
Feelies	8		★	★	★
Fish Pond	36		★	★	★
Follow the Leader	24		★	★	★
Forfeits	46		★	★	★
Game of the Poet	118			★	★
Grasshopper Contest	63	★	★		
Great Guggenheim	118			★	★
Group Art	112	★	★		
Group Lit	113		★	★	★
Guggenheim	115		★	★	★
Ha-Ha-Ha	68		★	★	★
Hair Ribbon Relay	97		★	★	★
Hilarious Handkerchief	69		★	★	★
Horse Race	48	★	★	★	★
Hot Potato	41	★	★	★	★
Hot Potato Spuds	76		★	★	★
Hul Gul	9		★	★	★
I Took a Trip	72		★	★	★
I Went to the City	71		★	★	★
In the Manner of the Word	57		★	★	★
In the Manner of the Word with Words	59			★	★
Japanese Crab Race	105		★	★	★
Laughing Ball	70		★	★	★
Lines	32	★	★	★	★
Losing Your Marbles	64		★	★	
Loose Caboose	83		★	★	★
Lottery	12	★	★	★	★
Magnetism	102		★	★	★
Marshmallow Race	66		★	★	
Mechanical Doll Race	102		★	★	★
Monkey See Monkey Do	74		★	★	★
Multiplication Dance	30			★	★
Murder	44		★	★	★
Musical Bumps	87	★	★		

AGE RANGE CHART & INDEX

Game	Page	Ages 6–8	8–12	13–18	Adult
Musical Chairs	86	★	★	★	★
Musical Grabs	23		★	★	★
Musical Islands	89			★	★
Noah's Ark	89		★	★	★
Number Line-Up	94		★	★	★
Nut Pitching	15	★	★	★	★
Odd Bean	9		★	★	★
One-Legged Contest	63	★	★	★	
Orange Race	96		★	★	★
Paper Training Race	66		★	★	
Phonies	123		★	★	★
Pinocchio Race	97		★	★	★
Poisoned Cushions	85		★	★	
Poor Pussy	69		★	★	★
Proverb Pairs	33		★	★	★
Riddle Pairs	32	★	★	★	★
Rumor	75	★	★	★	★
Salty Whistle Race	101	★	★	★	★
Sardines	84	★	★	★	★
Secret Words	121			★	★
Sherlock & Watson	93		★	★	★
Songs	34		★	★	★
Split Similes	37		★	★	★
Stalking Bigfoot	81		★	★	★
Suitcase Relay	99		★	★	★
Talk Fest	29		★	★	★
Teakettle	110		★	★	★
Terrible Twosomes	35	★	★	★	★
This Is My Nose	114	★	★	★	★
Truth or Consequences	42	★	★	★	★
Umbrella Bounce	18		★	★	★
Ummm!	77			★	★
Up Jenkins!	56		★	★	★
Who Am I?	28		★	★	★
William Tell Race	103		★	★	★
Zip Zap	21		★	★	★